A-level
Success

Physics

AQA

Practice Test Papers

Carol Tear

Contents

ACKNOWLEDGEMENTS

The author and publisher are grateful to the copyright holders for permission to use quoted materials and images.

Cover & P1: © Keith Publicover/Shutterstock.com

Every effort has been made to trace copyright holders and obtain their permission for the use of copyright material. The author and publisher will gladly receive information enabling them to rectify any error or omission in subsequent editions. All facts are correct at time of going to press.

Published by Letts Educational
An imprint of HarperCollins*Publishers*
1 London Bridge Street
London SE1 9GF

ISBN: 9780008179038

First published 2016

10 9 8 7 6 5 4 3 2

© HarperCollins*Publishers* Limited 2016

British Library Cataloguing in Publication Data.
A CIP record of this book is available from the British Library.

Series Concept and Development: Emily Linnett and Katherine Wilkinson
Author: Carol Tear
Commissioning and Series Editor: Chantal Addy
Editorial: Jill Laidlaw
Cover Design: Paul Oates
Inside Concept Design: Ian Wrigley
Text Design and Layout: Aptara®, inc.
Production: Lyndsey Rogers
Printed in China

MIX
Paper from responsible sources
FSC™ C007454

A-level
Physics
Practice paper for AQA

Paper 1

Time allowed: 2 hours

Materials

For this paper you must have:
- a pencil
- a ruler
- a calculator
- a data and formulae booklet.

Instructions
- Answer **all** questions.
- Show **all** your working.

Information
- The maximum mark for this paper is 85.

Name: ....

Section A

Answer **all** questions in this section.

---

0 1   A strange particle, the K^- kaon, reacts with a proton and forms a particle X and a K^+ kaon.

0 1 · 1 Write an equation for this reaction.

[1 mark]

....

0 1 · 2 Show that the charge of particle X is –1.

[1 mark]

....

....

0 1 · 3 Deduce the baryon number and strangeness of particle X.

[2 marks]

baryon number ....

strangeness ....

0 1 · 4 Determine the quark structure of particle X.

[3 marks]

quark structure ....

A student wants to find the resistance of component X, shown in **Figure 1**. There is no ohmmeter, but other electrical equipment is available. Complete this circuit diagram to show how you would measure the resistance of X.

[2 marks]

Figure 1

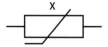

The student sets up the circuit in **Figure 2**, which contains component X.

Figure 2

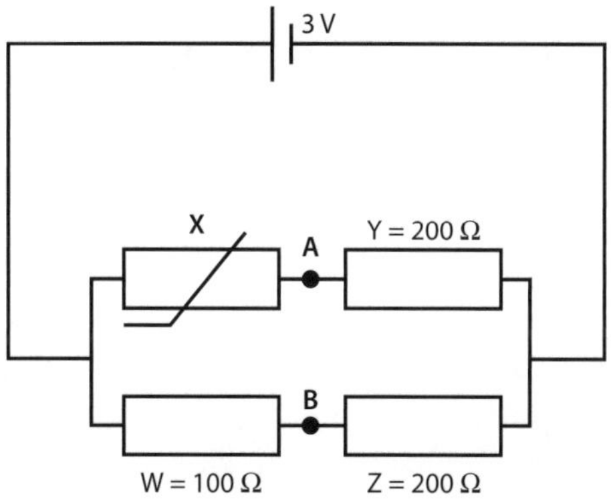

The resistance of X is 100 Ω.

0 2 · 2 Calculate the total resistance and the current in the circuit.

[4 marks]

resistance .... Ω

current .... mA

0 2 · 3 An ammeter is connected between points A and B. State and explain the current recorded by the ammeter.

[2 marks]

0 2 · 4 The resistance of component X decreases to 50 Ω.

Suggest why the resistance decreased. Explain your answer.

[2 marks]

0 2 · 5 State and explain the effect of this change on the current between A and B.

[3 marks]

| 0 3 | Gliders move along a horizontal linear air track with negligible friction supported by a cushion of air.

| 0 3 . 1 | A glider of mass 0.40 kg is moving with velocity 0.30 m s⁻¹ towards a stationary glider of mass 0.25 kg. The gliders collide and stick together. Show that their final velocity is about 0.2 m s⁻¹.

[3 marks]

| 0 3 . 2 | The gliders reach the end of the track and rebound from a fixed barrier, travelling back at the same speed. Determine the change in momentum when the gliders rebound.

[1 mark]

momentum .... kg m s⁻¹

| 0 3 . 3 | In the next experiment two gliders C and D each of mass 0.20 kg are travelling towards each other and make an elastic collision.

Compare and contrast an elastic collision and an inelastic collision.

[2 marks]

| 0 3 . 4 | The velocity of C is 0.30 m s⁻¹ and of D is −0.20 m s⁻¹. After collision the final velocity of D is 0.30 m s⁻¹. Calculate the final velocity of C and show whether the collision is elastic.

[5 marks]

final velocity of C .... m s⁻¹

elastic or inelastic? ....

| 0 4 | A spring is suspended vertically and extends 0.14 m when a mass of 0.31 kg is hung on its lower end.

| 0 4 . 1 | Show that the spring constant of the spring is about 20 N m⁻¹.

[2 marks]

| 0 4 . 2 | The spring is pulled down slightly and released so that it oscillates with simple harmonic motion about the equilibrium position with an amplitude of 0.025 m.

Calculate the period of the oscillation.

[1 mark]

period _____ s

| 0 4 . 3 | Explain at what point in the oscillation the tension in the spring will be at maximum value and calculate this maximum tension.

[3 marks]

_____

_____

_____

maximum tension _____ N

| 0 4 . 4 | The mass and spring are taken to the Moon. Vertical oscillations with the same amplitude are set up in exactly the same way. Without further calculation, comment on the changes, if any, that you would expect to the period of oscillation and the maximum tension.

[3 marks]

_____

_____

_____

| 0 5 | A marble of mass 6.0 g is rolled down the plastic track shown in **Figure 3**. Z is 0.10 m higher than Y. The path through Z is part of a circle of radius 0.75 m. Assume that friction is negligible.

Figure 3

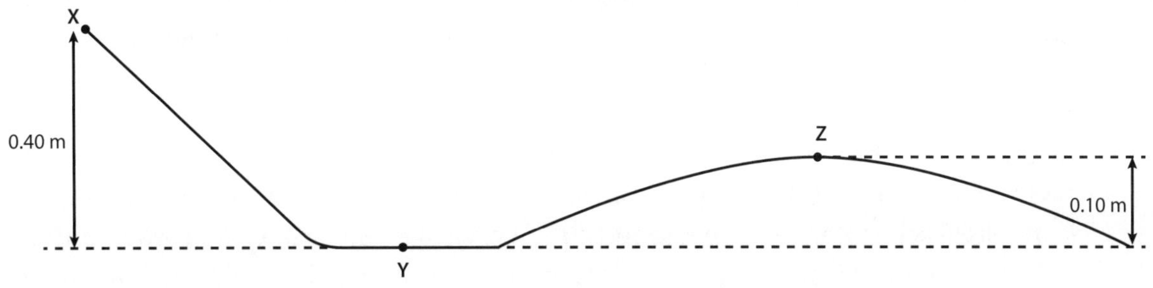

A marble is released at X, which is 0.40 m higher than Y.

| 0 5 |·| 1 | Calculate the speed of the marble at Y.

[2 marks]

speed .... m s⁻¹

| 0 5 |·| 2 | Calculate the speed of the marble at Z.

[2 marks]

speed .... m s⁻¹

| 0 5 |·| 3 | Draw a diagram showing the forces on the marble at Z and calculate the reaction between the track and the marble at Z.

[4 marks]

reaction .... N

Read through the following passage and answer the questions that follow it.

The invention of the blue LED

Light-emitting diode (LED) technology is based on electroluminescence, which is a
phenomenon discovered in 1907 by Henry Joseph Round. Electroluminescence is light
emitted when an electric current passes through a material. In 1955 Rubin Braunstein
reported that some simple semiconductor diodes emit radiation when current passes
5 through them, but it was not until 1961 that the first practical device – a pure gallium
arsenide (GaAs) crystal with a 900 nm wavelength output – was reported.

In 1962 Nick Holonyack developed the first visible red LED, with a wavelength of
660 nm. New semiconductor materials led to LEDs with other colours, but the blue
LED was more difficult to achieve. In 1979, Shuji Nakamura invented the first blue
10 LED using gallium nitride (GaN), but it was too expensive for commercial use. He
improved the design and in 1994 he invented the first low-cost bright blue LED.

The blue LED made white light possible because our eyes see a combination of red,
green and blue, or of yellow and blue, as white light. One way to make a white LED
is to use a phosphor coating to absorb some of the blue light and emit yellow light.
15 This results in a spectrum of yellow (maximum output at wavelength 580 nm) and
blue (maximum output at 450 nm), which we see as white light.

0 6 · 1 State the wavelength region of the electromagnetic spectrum of the radiation from the first
practical device (line 6).

[1 mark]

0 6 · 2 Show that the frequency of the first red LED (line 7) is 4.5×10^{-14} Hz and calculate the
energy of 1 photon in electronvolts.

[3 marks]

energy .... eV

0 6 . 3 Describe the process that takes place in an atom in the phosphor coating that produces yellow light (line 14).

[2 marks]

....

....

....

0 6 . 4 A student suggests that the red LED could be used with phosphor coatings that emit green light of wavelength 550 nm, and blue light of wavelength 450 nm to produce white light. Explain whether this is possible.

[2 marks]

....

....

....

0 6 . 5 The white light LED described in lines 13 to 16 is viewed using a spectrometer and a diffraction grating with 1500 lines per mm. Calculate the first order angle at which the centre of the blue line is seen.

[2 marks]

angle .... °

0 6 . 6 Describe the spectrum that would be seen with the spectrometer.

[2 marks]

....

....

....

END OF SECTION A

Section B

Each of questions **7** to **31** is followed by four responses, **A, B, C** and **D**. For each question select the best response.

Only **one** answer per question is allowed.

For each answer completely fill in the circle alongside the appropriate answer.

CORRECT METHOD [●]   WRONG METHODS [⊗] [⊙] [⊜] [✓]

If you want to change your answer, you must cross out your original answer as shown. [⊠]

If you wish to return to an answer previously crossed out, ring the answer you now wish to select as shown. [⊘]

---

0 7 A nucleus of $^{204}_{82}$Pb absorbs an alpha particle and emits a positron. What is the product nucleus?

[1 mark]

A $^{206}_{85}$At   ◯

B $^{208}_{85}$At   ◯

C $^{208}_{83}$Bi   ◯

D $^{207}_{84}$Po   ◯

0 8 The drag force F on a spherical object of radius r falling with terminal velocity v is given by:

$$F = 6\pi\eta rv$$

What are the units of η?

[1 mark]

A kg m^{-1} ◯

B kg m^{-1} s^{-1} ◯

C kg m^2 s^{-1} ◯

D m s^{-2} kg^{-1} ◯

0 9 A metal sheet is placed in a beam of electromagnetic radiation. Photoelectrons are emitted from the surface of the metal. Which list contains all the factors that determine the maximum speed of the emitted electrons?

[1 mark]

A The frequency of the electromagnetic radiation.

B The frequency and the intensity of the electromagnetic radiation.

C The frequency of the electromagnetic radiation and the work function of the metal.

D The frequency and the intensity of the electromagnetic radiation and the work function of the metal.

1 0 The diagram shows three energy levels for the outermost electron in an atom. λ_A λ_B and λ_C are the wavelengths of the photons emitted when the electrons drop from one energy level to another.

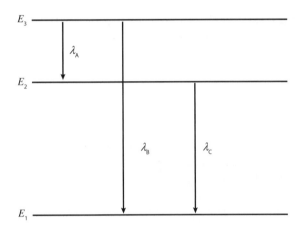

Which of the following statements is correct?

[1 mark]

A $\lambda_B = \lambda_A + \lambda_C$

B If λ_A is in the visible region, then λ_C could be in the infrared region.

C The frequency of the radiation with wavelength λ_A is less than the frequency of the radiation with wavelength λ_B.

D If λ_B is in the visible region, then λ_A could be in the ultraviolet region.

1 1 The diameter of a sphere is measured to be 0.025 (±0.001) m. The volume of the sphere is correctly calculated to be

$$V = \frac{4\pi}{3}\left(\frac{d}{2}\right)^3 = 8.81 \times 10^{-6}\,\text{m}$$

How should the percentage uncertainty in the volume, resulting from the uncertainty in the diameter, be calculated?

[1 mark]

A $\dfrac{0.001}{0.025} \times 100\%$ ⬭

B $3 \times \dfrac{0.001}{0.025} \times 100\%$ ⬭

C $\dfrac{0.001}{8.181 \times 10^{-6}} \times 100\%$ ⬭

D $3 \times \dfrac{0.001}{8.181 \times 10^{-6}} \times 100\%$ ⬭

1 2 Considering the alpha particle, the proton and the positron, which particle has the largest charge-to-mass ratio and which has the smallest?

[1 mark]

	Largest charge-to-mass ratio, Q/m	Smallest charge-to-mass ratio, Q/m	
A	alpha particle	positron	⬭
B	positron	alpha particle	⬭
C	positron	proton	⬭
D	proton	alpha particle	⬭

1 3 The frequency of the first harmonic of a string fixed at both ends is 200 Hz. The tension in the wire is doubled. What is the new fundamental frequency?

[1 mark]

A   283 Hz

B   141 Hz

C   400 Hz

D   800 Hz

1 4 A wire with resistance R and length l has a circular cross-section with diameter d. A second wire with resistance R is made of the same material and has a square cross-section of side d. What is the length of this second wire?

[1 mark]

A $2\pi l$

B $\dfrac{2l}{\pi}$

C $4\pi l$

D $\dfrac{4l}{\pi}$

1 5 A beam of light passes through a polarising filter with its axis of polarisation at 0° and a second polarising filter with its axis of polarisation at 90°. No light is transmitted. A third polarising filter is placed between the two crossed filters and rotated through 360°.

As the third filter is rotated, which of the following is true?

[1 mark]

A   No light is transmitted at any angle.

B   Some light is transmitted at all angles.

C   Some light is transmitted, but only when the third filter has its axis of polarisation at 0°, 45°, 225° or 315°.

D   Some light is transmitted whenever the axis of polarisation of the third filter is not 0° or is a multiple of 90°.

1 6 A light ray incident on the cladding of an optical fibre refracts along the core-cladding boundary as shown.

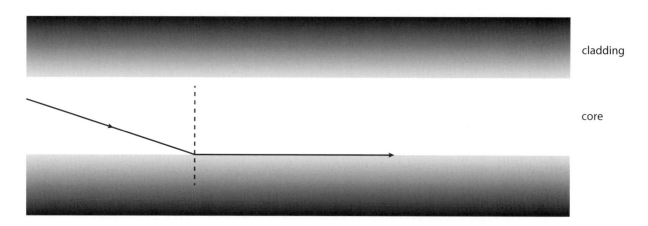

What is the critical angle at the boundary between the core and the cladding?

speed of light in the core = 2.02×10^8 m s^{-1}

speed of light in the cladding = 2.08×10^8 m s^{-1}

[1 mark]

A 14° ⬭

B 42° ⬭

C 44° ⬭

D 76° ⬭

1 7 An experiment in which microwaves pass through two narrow slits is done in a vacuum.

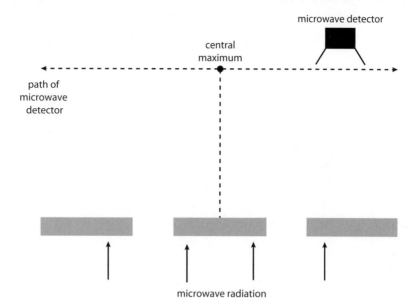

The slits act as coherent sources. The microwave detector is moved along the path shown. There is a central maximum intensity. On either side there are evenly spaced intensity maxima and minima.

When the microwave frequency is halved, what change in the pattern is observed?

[1 mark]

A   The pattern is unchanged.

B   The spacing of the maxima is unchanged,
but there is a central minimum.

C   The spacing of the maxima is doubled.

D   The spacing of the maxima is halved.

1 8 A uniform 1.0 m beam of weight W is supported on a pillar 10 cm from one end and by a rope attached 30 cm from the other end.

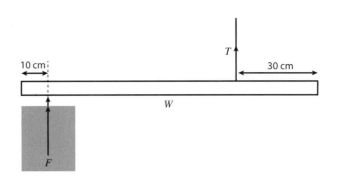

The reaction force from the pillar is F and the tension in the rope is T.

What is the ratio $T:F$?

[1 mark]

A 1:3

B 1:2

C 2:1

D 3:1

1 9 Three forces A, B and C act on the rim of a disc. Forces A and B are both 10 N and form a couple. Which diagram shows the correct force C for the disc to be in equilibrium?

[1 mark]

A   B   C   D

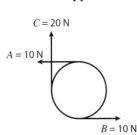 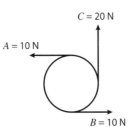 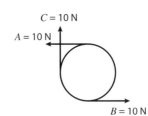 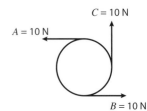

A

B

C

D

2 0 An object of mass 0.5 kg moves due South on a horizontal frictionless table with a speed of 3 m s⁻¹. A constant force 0.2 N due East acts on it for 10 s. What is the resultant velocity of the object?

[1 mark]

A 3.6 m s⁻¹ due East ⬭

B 3.6 m s⁻¹ 53° East of South ⬭

C 5 m s⁻¹ due East ⬭

D 5 m s⁻¹ 53° East of South ⬭

2 1 Two identical springs with spring constant k can be joined in parallel or in series.

 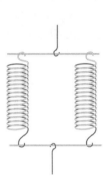

Which line of the table correctly shows the spring constant in each case?

[1 mark]

	Series combination	Parallel combination	
A	$2k$	$2k$	⬭
B	$2k$	$\dfrac{k}{2}$	⬭
C	$\dfrac{k}{2}$	$2k$	⬭
D	$\dfrac{k}{2}$	$\dfrac{k}{2}$	⬭

2 2 Two spheres of equal volume, one plastic and one metal, are projected horizontally from the top of a tall building at the same time and with the same velocity. Air resistance is negligible. Which statement correctly describes when and where they will land?

[1 mark]

A The metal sphere will land first and closer to the building.

B The metal sphere will land first and further from the building.

C The plastic sphere will land first and closer to the building.

D They will both land at the same time and at the same distance from the building.

2 3 Two projectiles P and Q are projected upwards at an angle with the same velocity v. The ground is horizontal. Projectile P is projected at angle θ to the horizontal and projectile Q at angle $(90° - \theta)$ to the horizontal. The time of flight of projectile P is t_p. What is the time of flight of projectile Q?

[1 mark]

A t_p

B $t_p \tan \theta$

C $\dfrac{t_p}{\tan \theta}$

D $t_p \dfrac{2v}{g} \tan \theta$

2 4 A person travels up and down in a lift, stopping at each floor of the building. Which statement about the reaction force from the floor on the person is true?

[1 mark]

Compared to the reaction force when the lift is stationary:

A the reaction force is greater when the lift is going down and slowing down.

B the reaction force is greater when the lift is going down and speeding up.

C the reaction force is greater when the lift is going up and slowing down.

D the reaction force is less when the lift is going up and speeding up.

2 5 A rope is used to raise a large crate of mass M to a platform at a height h above the ground. A ramp with negligible friction is set up at an angle of 45°, so that the rope can be used to pull the same mass up the ramp from the ground to the platform. What effect will this have on the work done in raising the crate?

[1 mark]

A   The work done will be less.

B   The work done will be more.

C   The work done will be the same.

D   The work done will depend on how quickly the crate is raised.

2 6 A crane motor X raises 30 kg a height of 120 m in 2 minutes. A winch motor Y raises 8 kg a height of 6 m in 1.5 s and a lift motor Z raises 4 kg a height of 15 m in 10 s. Which motor delivers the most output power?

[1 mark]

A   crane X

B   winch Y

C   lift Z

D   They are all the same.

2 7 In an open circuit the potential difference across the terminals of a cell is 9.0 V and when a current of 1.5 A passes through it is 7.8 V. What is the internal resistance of the cell?

[1 mark]

A   0.8 Ω

B   1.8 Ω

C   5.2 Ω

D   6.0 Ω

2 8 This circuit is used to operate a light switch.

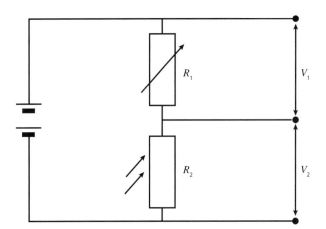

Which of the following statements correctly describes what happens as the amount of light and the resistance of R_1 is changed?

[1 mark]

A It gets dark, V_1 increases and can be used to switch on a lamp.
When R_1 is decreased it is darker before the lamp switches on.

B It gets dark, V_1 increases and can be used to switch on a lamp.
When R_1 is increased it is darker before the lamp switches on.

C It gets dark, V_2 increases and can be used to switch on a lamp.
When R_1 is decreased it is darker before the lamp switches on.

D It gets dark, V_2 increases and can be used to switch on a lamp.
When R_1 is increased it is darker before the lamp switches on.

2 9 A simple pendulum consisting of a small mass on the end of an inextensible string swings with simple harmonic motion. Which of the following statements correctly describes the energy in the system?

[1 mark]

A The energy is at its maximum as the object passes through the mid-point of the oscillation. ☐

B The energy is at its minimum as the object passes through the mid-point of the oscillation. ☐

C The energy is at its maximum as the object reaches the highest point of the oscillation. ☐

D The energy will not change with the position of the object. ☐

3 0 An object oscillates with damped simple harmonic motion. Which of the following statements about the damping force is true?

[1 mark]

A It is always in the opposite direction to the displacement. ☐

B It is always in the opposite direction to the velocity. ☐

C It is always proportional to the displacement. ☐

D It is always in the same direction as the acceleration. ☐

3 **1** An object travels around a circle with radius r. The centre of the circle is at O.

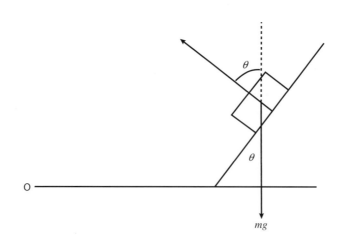

The edge of the circle is banked at an angle θ so that, at speed, v, the object cannot slip. What is the value of tan θ?

[1 mark]

A $\dfrac{mg}{rv^2}$ ⬭

B $\dfrac{rg}{v^2}$ ⬭

C $\dfrac{rv^2}{mg}$ ⬭

D $\dfrac{v^2}{rg}$ ⬭

END OF QUESTIONS

A-level
Physics

Practice paper for AQA

Paper 2

Time allowed: 2 hours

Materials

For this paper you must have:
- a pencil
- a ruler
- a calculator
- a data and formulae booklet.

Instructions
- Answer **all** questions.
- Show **all** your working.

Information
- The maximum mark for this paper is 85.

Name: ....

Section A

Answer **all** questions in this section.

---

0 1   A solid 'phase change material' (PCM) that melts at 37 °C is used where incubators are unavailable to keep small babies at the right body temperature of 37 °C.

In a test 400 g of the PCM is heated from 15 °C until it is all molten and its temperature has increased to 39 °C. The test is done in an insulated glass container with mass 240 g and specific heat capacity 840 J kg^{-1} K^{-1}. The thermal energy transferred to or from the surroundings during the test is negligible.

Table 1 shows some technical data for the PCM.

Table 1

Melting point	37 °C
Specific heat capacity when solid	2200 J kg^{-1} K^{-1}
Specific heat capacity when liquid	2600 J kg^{-1} K^{-1}

0 1 . 1 Calculate the thermal energy required to raise the temperature of the PCM **and** the container to 37 °C.

[2 marks]

energy .... J

0 1 · 2 The 12 V heating element used had a current of 1.7 A and took 90 minutes to raise the temperature of the PCM and the container to 39 °C. Determine the latent heat of fusion of the PCM.

[4 marks]

latent heat of fusion .... J/kg

0 1 · 3 In use, the PCM is enclosed in a quilt – it is heated so that it has partially melted and the quilt is wrapped around the baby. Suggest how this helps stabilise the baby's body temperature.

[1 mark]

_____

_____

_____

0 2 · 1 A student writes, "The gas laws are empirical. Kinetic theory is theoretical." Explain what these statements mean.

[2 marks]

1. ....

....

2. ....

....

0 2 · 2 Kinetic theory assumes that the pressure of an ideal gas of molecules of mass m is

$$p = \frac{1}{3}\frac{Nm}{V}(C_{rms})^2$$

State the physical significance of $\frac{Nm}{V}$ and explain your answer.

[2 marks]

....

....

....

0 2 . 3 Show how $(C_{rms})^2$ is calculated for four particles with velocity v_1, v_2, v_3 and v_4.

[1 mark]

0 2 . 4 The rms speed of nitrogen molecules is 520 m s^{-1}. Determine the temperature of the nitrogen gas.

(Relative molecular mass of N_2 = 28)

[3 marks]

temperature .... K

0 3 . 1 The electron and the proton in a hydrogen atom are separated by a mean distance of about 5.3×10^{-11} m. Calculate the ratio of the magnitudes of the electrostatic force and the gravitational force between the two particles and comment on the effect of the gravitational force on subatomic particles.

[4 marks]

0 3 . 2 You have compared the magnitudes of the forces, now compare and contrast other features of gravitational and electrostatic fields.

[5 marks]

0 4   A copper sheet is held between the two poles of an electromagnet, as shown in **Figure 1**.

Figure 1

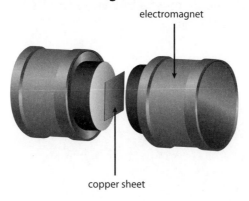

An alternating current flows through the coils of the electromagnet.

0 4 . 1 Explain why the temperature of the sheet increases.

[4 marks]

0 4 . 2 State **two** ways of increasing the rate of heating without changing or moving the sheet. Explain your answers.

[2 marks]

1. ....

   ....

2. ....

   ....

0 4 . 3 The sheet is replaced with a sheet of the same size and shape but made of a metal with higher resistance. Explain how the rate of heating is changed.

[2 marks]

| 0 5 | A cyclotron, shown in **Figure 2**, is a device for accelerating charged particles. It has two D-shaped containers where there is a magnetic field, provided by magnetic poles above and below the Ds. Across the 2 cm gap between the Ds there is an alternating electric field. There is no electric field in the Ds.

Figure 2

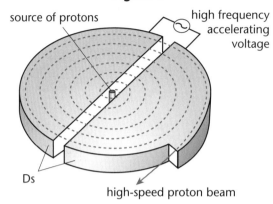

| 0 5 · 1 | The source at the centre of the gap releases protons that are accelerated and enter the first D. The voltage across the gap is 10 kV. Show that the initial force on the proton is 8×10^{-14} N. (Assume the electric field across the gap is uniform.)

[2 marks]

| 0 5 · 2 | A proton starts at rest at the centre of the gap and is accelerated to the first D. Show that its acceleration is about 5×10^{13} m s^{-2} **and** that when it enters the D for the first time its speed is about 1×10^6 m s^{-1}.

[3 marks]

0 5 . 3 The proton enters the first D and starts making a number of laps around the Ds.

It is accelerated across the 2 cm gap twice on each lap. It travels at constant speed in the Ds.

This makes a total distance over which it is accelerated of ($2n \times 2.0$) cm, where n is the number of laps.

Calculate the number of laps to reach 10% of the speed of light.

[3 marks]

number of laps, n ....

0 5 . 4 Inside the Ds the protons are in the vertical magnetic field and move in a circular path. On **Figure 2** mark a proton inside a D on one of the dotted paths and draw labelled arrows showing the direction of the force on the proton and its direction of motion. State the direction of the magnetic field and deduce which pole of the magnet is a north pole.

[2 marks]

0 5 . 5 By considering the magnetic force on the proton moving it in a circular path show that the radius of the path r is

$$r = \frac{mv}{Be}$$

where m is the mass and e the charge on the proton, v is its velocity and B is the magnetic field.

[2 marks]

0 5 . 6 Before the proton source is opened, the inside of the cyclotron is a vacuum. Suggest why a vacuum is required.

[1 mark]

Read through the following passage and answer the questions that follow it.

Many space probes use radioisotope thermoelectric generators (RTGs). In an RTG, radioactive decay transfers energy by heating the surroundings. It can be used to warm the electronics, or to generate electricity. The radioisotope used by NASA is plutonium-238, which is contained in pellets of plutonium dioxide. Plutonium-238
5 has a half-life of 88 years.

RTGs were used in the 1970s to power the Voyager and Pioneer deep-space probes that have now left the solar system. The Curiosity rover that explored Mars in 2012 had an RTG containing about 4 kg of plutonium to provide power and keep the electronics warm. (On Mars temperatures range from −133 °C to 27 °C and there are
10 strong winds and dust storms.) It was designed to last for one Mars year (687 Earth days). Previous rovers have used some radioisotope heating, but relied on solar panels for their power.

In an RTG electricity is generated using a thermoelectric effect. A temperature difference is used to generate a potential difference and this is used to charge two
15 rechargeable lithium-ion batteries.

The United States stopped producing plutonium-238 in 1988 and instead purchased it from Russia. Russia has now also stopped production and stocks are running low. In December 2015 the USA reported producing 50 g of plutonium-238 from neptunium-238 and they plan to increase production to about 1.5 kg a year.

0 6 . 1 Plutonium-238, $^{238}_{94}$Pu, decays to uranium-234, releasing an alpha particle.

Use the data in **Table 2** to calculate the energy released in joules by the decay of 1 nucleus of plutonium-238.

[3 marks]

Table 2

Nucleus	Mass/u
plutonium-238	238.04955
uranium-234	234.043924
helium-4	4.00151

energy _____ J

0 6 · 2 Show that the number of atoms, N, in 4.3 kg of pure plutonium-238 is about 1×10^{25}.

[1 mark]

number of atoms, N ....

0 6 · 3 Use information about plutonium-238 (line 4) to calculate the initial activity of 4 kg of plutonium-238.

[2 marks]

activity .... Bq

0 6 · 4 Determine the initial power output of the RTG.

[1 mark]

power .... W

0 6 · 5 Suggest and explain the advantages of using RTGs instead of solar panels for powering deep-space probes and Mars rovers.

[2 marks]

....

....

....

....

0 6 · 6 Use the equation for the gravitational attraction between the Sun and a planet to show that $T^2 \propto r^3$, where T is the period and r the radius of orbit of a planet around the Sun.

[3 marks]

0 6 · 7 Using the information in lines 10–11, determine the ratio between the radii of the orbits of Mars and the Earth, $r_M{:}r_E$ and calculate the radius of the Mars orbit, r_M.

Earth's radius of orbit, $r_E = 1.50 \times 10^{11}$ m

[3 marks]

ratio ....

radius .... m

END OF SECTION A

Section B

Each of questions **7** to **31** is followed by four responses, **A, B, C** and **D**. For each question select the best response.

Only **one** answer per question is allowed.

For each answer completely fill in the circle alongside the appropriate answer.

CORRECT METHOD   WRONG METHODS

If you want to change your answer, you must cross out your original answer as shown.

If you wish to return to an answer previously crossed out, ring the answer you now wish to select as shown.

---

0 7 A fixed mass of gas occupies a constant volume. The temperature is T in degrees Celsius. The pressure p is doubled. What is the new temperature in degrees Celsius?

[1 mark]

A $2T$ ⬭

B $\frac{1}{2}T$ ⬭

C $2T + 273$ ⬭

D $\frac{T - 273}{2}$ ⬭

0 8 Which statement is true for an ideal gas?

[1 mark]

A   The average internal energy of the atoms is zero.   ⬭

B   The internal energy decreases when work is done on the gas.   ⬭

C   The internal energy equals the average kinetic energy of the atoms.   ⬭

D   The internal energy equals the average potential energy of the atoms.   ⬭

0 9 Which graph correctly shows how the gravitational force, F, between two masses varies with the distance between them, r?

[1 mark]

A

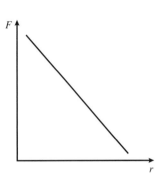

B

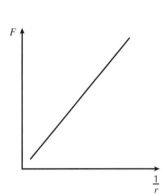

C

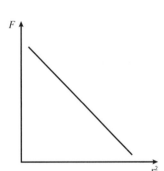

D

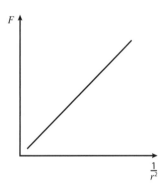

A

B

C

D

1 0 Which statement correctly defines the gravitational potential at a point in a gravitational field?

[1 mark]

A The work done in moving any mass from infinity to that point.

B The work done in moving any mass to infinity from that point.

C The work done in moving a unit mass from infinity to that point.

D The work done in moving a unit mass to infinity from that point.

1 1 Jupiter has a radius about 11 times that of the Earth, and a mass of about 320 times that of the Earth. The gravitational potential at the Earth's surface is -6.3×10^7 J kg^{-1}. What is the approximate value of the gravitational potential at the surface of Jupiter?

[1 mark]

A -1.8×10^9 J kg^{-1} ⬭

B -1.7×10^8 J kg^{-1} ⬭

C -2.4×10^7 J kg^{-1} ⬭

D -2.2×10^6 J kg^{-1} ⬭

1 2 A point X is a distance $3r$ from a large point mass $3M$. The gravitational potential at X is V. A second large point mass $10M$ is placed a distance $4r$ from the first mass and $5r$ from point X. What is the new value of the gravitational potential at X?

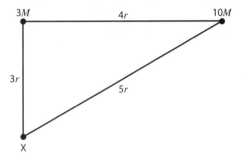

[1 mark]

A $\dfrac{11V}{15}$ ⬭

B $2V$ ⬭

C $3V$ ⬭

D $\dfrac{23V}{3}$ ⬭

1 3 Which line of the table is correct for a geostationary satellite and a geosynchronous satellite of the Earth?

[1 mark]

		Geostationary	Geosynchronous	
A		Orbital period is always one day. Plane of orbit is always the equatorial plane.	Orbital period is always one day. Stays over a fixed point on the Earth.	○
B		Orbital period is always one day. Stays over a fixed point on the Earth.	Orbital period is always one day. Plane of orbit is always the equatorial plane.	○
C		Orbital period is always one day. Plane of orbit is always the equatorial plane. Stays over a fixed point on the Earth.	Orbital period is always one day.	○
D		Orbital period is always one day. Stays over a fixed point on the Earth.	Orbital period is always one day. Plane of orbit is always the equatorial plane.	○

1 4 Two particles are a distance d apart. One has a charge of $+Q$ and the other has a charge of $-4Q$. The attractive force between them $= F$.

$+Q$ ———————— d ———————— $-4Q$

The particles are moved closer together so that the distance between them is $\frac{1}{2}d$. Both particles are given an additional charge of $+Q$. What is the new force between the particles?

[1 mark]

A 2.5F ○

B 3F ○

C 5F ○

D 6F ○

Electrons in a vacuum start from rest and are accelerated through a potential difference V. Which graph shows how their velocity v varies with the potential difference?

[1 mark]

A

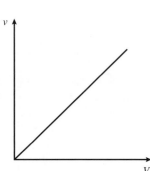

B

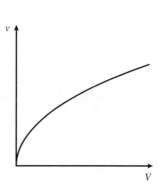

C

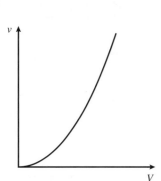

D

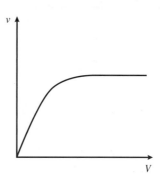

A

B

C

D

1 6 Two parallel metal plates 50 mm apart are charged so that one has a potential of 500 V and the other a potential of 0 V. There is a uniform field between them. The position of points X, Y and Z are shown on the diagram. Which line of the table correctly shows the work done in moving an electron from point X to point Y and from point X to point Z?

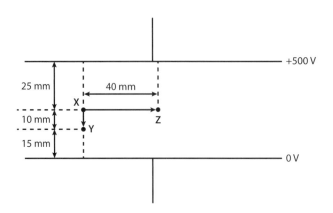

[1 mark]

	Work done moving from X to Y/J	Work done moving from X to Z/J	
A	1.6×10^{-16}	0	⬭
B	1.6×10^{-17}	0	⬭
C	1.6×10^{-16}	1.6×10^{-15}	⬭
D	1.6×10^{-17}	1.6×10^{-15}	⬭

1 7 A parallel plate capacitor with an air gap has capacitance C. It is connected to a battery with potential difference V so that there is a charge Q on the capacitor and it stores energy E. The air gap is gradually filled with oil that has a relative permittivity of 2, while the capacitor is still connected to the battery. What will happen to the charge on the capacitor and the energy stored by the capacitor?

[1 mark]

	New charge on capacitor	New energy stored by capacitor	
A	$\dfrac{Q}{2}$	$\dfrac{E}{4}$	⬭
B	$\dfrac{Q}{2}$	$\dfrac{E}{2}$	⬭
C	$2Q$	$2E$	⬭
D	$2Q$	$4E$	⬭

1 8 A charged capacitor is discharged through a resistor. Data is collected for the potential difference V across the capacitor at a number of times t after the start of the discharge. Which variables should be plotted to give a graph with a straight line?

[1 mark]

A V against t ⬭

B V against $\dfrac{1}{t}$ ⬭

C V against $\ln t$ ⬭

D $\ln V$ against t ⬭

1 9 The charge on a fully charged capacitor is 10 μC. It is discharged through a resistor. The time constant of the circuit is 47 s. What is the charge remaining after 47 s?

[1 mark]

A   0.21 μC   ⬭

B   3.7 μC   ⬭

C   3.9 μC   ⬭

D   5.0 μC   ⬭

2 0 The S.I. unit for magnetic flux density is the tesla (T). What is 1 T in base units?

[1 mark]

A   1 kg A m   ⬭

B   1 kg A^{-1} s^{-2} ⬭

C   1 kg A m s^{-2} ⬭

D   1 kg A^{-1} m s^{-2} ⬭

2 1 A square coil of side l with N turns is placed in a uniform magnetic field B so that its plane is perpendicular to the field. The coil is replaced with a square coil with sides $l/2$ and $2N$ turns. What is the new flux linkage?

[1 mark]

A Half the original flux linkage.

B The same as the original flux linkage.

C Double the original flux linkage.

D Four times the original flux linkage.

2 2 An aircraft is flying perpendicular to the Earth's magnetic field at a place where the field is 5.0×10^{-5} T. It has a wingspan of 25 m and is flying at 125 m s^{-1}. What is the induced emf in the wing?

[1 mark]

A 1.6×10^{-8} V

B 1.0×10^{-5} V

C 2.5×10^{-4} V

D 0.16 V

2 3 What is the root mean square value of a sinusoidal alternating current?

[1 mark]

A $\sqrt{2}$ (the mean value of the current over a half cycle)

B $\sqrt{2}$ (the peak value of the current)

C $\dfrac{1}{\sqrt{2}}$ (the mean value of the current over a half cycle)

D $\dfrac{1}{\sqrt{2}}$ (the peak value of the current)

2 4 A step-down transformer is used with the mains to supply a low voltage. A replacement is required to give the same input and output voltages and improved efficiency. Which of the following changes would increase the efficiency of the transformer?

[1 mark]

A Improve the insulation of the wire used to make the coils.   ○

B Increase the number of turns in the primary coil.   ○

C Increase the number of turns in the secondary coil.   ○

D Replace the solid iron core with one made of layers of iron.   ○

2 5 In the alpha particle scattering experiment, alpha particles are scattered from gold foil. What model of the atom is suggested by the results of the experiment?

[1 mark]

A The atom has a nucleus of large radius and high density.   ○

B The atom has a nucleus of large radius and low density.   ○

C The atom has a nucleus of small radius and high density.   ○

D The atom has a nucleus of small radius and low density.   ○

2 6 At a certain time a radioactive sample X contains N radioactive nuclides with a half-life $T_{1/2}$ and a second radioactive sample Y contains $2N$ radioactive nuclides with half-life $3\,T_{1/2}$. The activity of sample X is A. What is the activity of sample Y?

[1 mark]

A $\dfrac{2}{3}A$ ○

B $\dfrac{3}{2}A$ ○

C $6A$ ○

D $\dfrac{1}{6}A$ ○

2 7 Before measuring the count rate of a radioactive source, a student measures the background count in the laboratory. What causes this background radiation?

[1 mark]

   A The radioactive decay of naturally occurring radioactive isotopes and those formed by human activities as well as radiation from space. ⬭

   B The radioactive decay of radioactive isotopes formed by human activities. ⬭

   C The radioactive decay of naturally occurring radioactive isotopes not affected by human activities. ⬭

   D The radiation left over from the Big Bang at the start of the Universe. ⬭

2 8 The radioactive decay constant of a free neutron is 1.13 $(ms)^{-1}$. What percentage of a large number of free neutrons will still remain after 15 minutes?

[1 mark]

   A 0% ⬭

   B 36% ⬭

   C 64% ⬭

   D 98% ⬭

2 9 How does the density of the nucleus depend on the number of nucleons forming the nucleus?

[1 mark]

   A It is directly proportional to the number of nucleons in the nucleus. ⬭

   B It is directly proportional to the number of protons in the nucleus. ⬭

   C It is independent of the number of nucleons in the nucleus. ⬭

   D It is inversely proportional to the number of nucleons in the nucleus. ⬭

3 0 This table shows some suggestions of how the binding energy per nucleon of the product changes compared to the initial nuclide, when nuclear fusion and nuclear fission occur. Which line of the table is correct?

[1 mark]

	Binding energy per nucleon when nuclear fusion occurs	Binding energy per nucleon when nuclear fission occurs	
A	decreases	decreases	⬭
B	decreases	increases	⬭
C	increases	decreases	⬭
D	increases	increases	⬭

3 1 The table shows some factors to be considered when choosing materials for use in a nuclear reactor. Which line of the table correctly shows the most important factors to be considered for the moderator, the control rods and the coolant for the reactor?

[1 mark]

	High number of interactions between neutron and material	Neutrons are absorbed and resulting nuclide fissions	Good absorber of neutrons	High specific heat capacity	
A	coolant	moderator		control rods	⬭
B	control rods	coolant	moderator		⬭
C	moderator		control rods	coolant	⬭
D		moderator	coolant	control rods	⬭

END OF QUESTIONS

A-level
Physics
Practice paper for AQA

Paper 3 – Section A

Materials

For this paper you must have:

- a pencil
- a ruler
- a calculator
- a data and formulae booklet
- a question paper/answer book for Section B.

Instructions
- Answer **all** questions.
- Show **all** your working.
- The total time for both sections of this paper is 2 hours.

Information
- The maximum mark for this section is 45.

Name: ....

Section A

Answer **all** questions in this section.

---

0 1   A student carries out an experiment to measure the Young modulus of a metal wire.

0 1 · 1 List **two** safety precautions the student should take while doing this experiment and explain why they are necessary.

[3 marks]

....

....

....

....

....

0 1 · 2 State the name of an instrument that a student could use to accurately measure the diameter of the wire.

[1 mark]

....

0 1 · 3 **Table 1** shows three measurements of the diameter.

Table 1

	First reading	Second reading	Third reading
Diameter of wire d/mm	0.77	0.77	0.79

Calculate the mean diameter of the wire **and** the absolute uncertainty in the measurement.

[2 marks]

diameter of wire .... $\pm$ .... mm

0 1 · 4 Calculate the cross-sectional area of the wire in metres² **and** its percentage uncertainty.

[3 marks]

cross-sectional area of wire .... m² ± .... %

0 1 · 5 The student wants to plot a stress–strain graph. List the measurements the student must make to calculate values for stress and strain.

[3 marks]

....

....

....

0 1 · 6 **Figure 1** shows the graph that the student plotted of stress against strain.

Figure 1

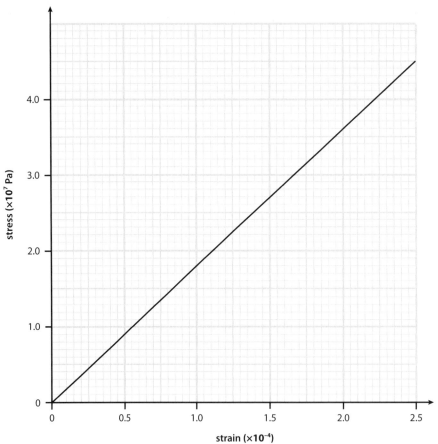

Use the graph to calculate the value of the Young modulus.

[3 marks]

Young modulus .... Pa

| 0 2 | The value of the acceleration due to gravity, g, can be determined by using a simple pendulum.

The equation is $T = 2\pi\sqrt{\dfrac{l}{g}}$.

A student times the swings of a mass hanging from a string and measures the length of the string. The experiment is repeated with different lengths of string.

| 0 2 · 1 | Explain why the student swings the pendulum through a very small angle.

[1 mark]

| 0 2 · 2 | **Table 2** shows the student's results.

Table 2

Length, l/m	Time for 10 swings/s	Period, T/s
0.8	18.4	1.84
1.0	20	2.0
1.1	21.4	2.14
1.2	23	2.3

Comment on these results, and suggest how you would improve them.

[4 marks]

0 2 · 3 The student measured the 10 swings using a stopwatch. Outline the method you would use to do this accurately.

[2 marks]

0 2 · 4 The student:
- calculates values of T^2
- plots a graph of T^2 against l
- draws a straight line of best fit through the origin
- measures the gradient of the graph to be 4.2 s² m⁻¹.

Show that for motion described by the equation in 02 the graph of T^2 against l is a straight line through the origin and calculate a value for g.

[3 marks]

acceleration due to gravity, g .... m s⁻²

Another student carries out the same experiment with the arrangement shown in **Figure 2** to measure the length of the pendulum.

Figure 2

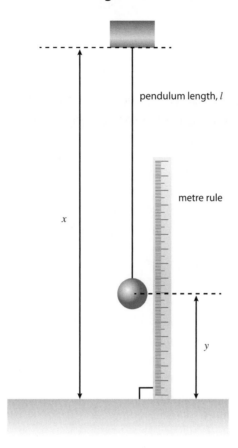

The length x is measured as at the start of the experiment and has an uncertainty of ± 2 mm. The length y is measured with a standard metre ruler marked in millimetres.

The length of the pendulum $l = x - y$.

0 2 . 5 Estimate the uncertainty in the length of the pendulum as a result of using these measuring instruments. Explain your answer.

[2 marks]

uncertainty in l = ±.. mm

0 2 · 6 Due to a mistake, the recorded measurement of x is 2 cm too large, leading to an error in the measured pendulum lengths.

State the name given to this type of error.

[1 mark]

0 2 · 7 Without further calculation, describe the effect this error has on the graph the student plots **and** on the value of g calculated from the graph.

[2 marks]

0 3 Boyle's law states that the volume of a fixed mass of gas is inversely proportional to the pressure applied to it if the temperature is kept constant.

Figure 3 shows an experiment to test the law.

Figure 3

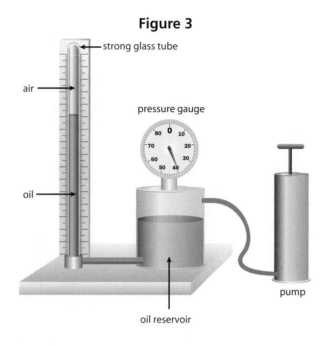

The pump is used to raise the pressure on the air in the tube.

0 3 . 1 State and explain **one** safety precaution you would take when using this equipment.

[2 marks]

_____

_____

0 3 . 2 Explain why it is important to wait between increasing the pressure and reading the volume.

[1 mark]

_____

_____

0 3 . 3 Describe how you would make sure that you read the volume scale accurately.

[1 mark]

_____

Table 3 shows results from the experiment.

Table 3

Pressure p/x 10⁵ Pa	Volume V/cm³		
1.0	40.0		
1.4	29.0		
1.8	22.0		
2.2	18.0		
2.5	16.0		
3.0	13.0		

0 3 · 4 You are to show whether Boyle's law is true for this gas by plotting a suitable graph.

Make any calculations that you need in order to plot your graph. The columns in **Table 3** are for you to use to calculate and tabulate the derived data that you need.

[3 marks]

0 3 . 5 Plot your graph on **Figure 4**. The values of p are provided on the x axis.

Figure 4

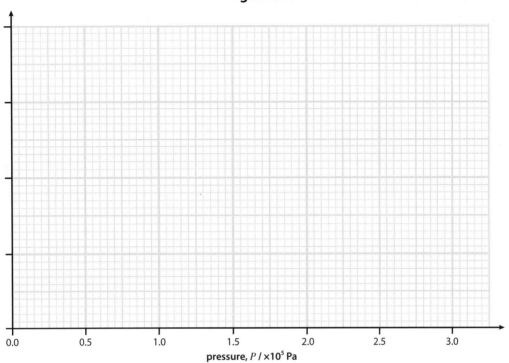

pressure, P / ×10⁵ Pa

[3 marks]

0 3 . 6 Comment on whether Boyle's law is true for this gas.

[1 mark]

....

....

0 3 . 7 Charles' law states that the volume of a fixed mass of gas at constant pressure is proportional to temperature measured in kelvin.

Describe an experiment to demonstrate Charles' law. Include in your answer:
- a description of the equipment (which may include a diagram)
- an outline of the procedure
- an explanation of how you would use the data to demonstrate whether Charles' law is true for the gas.

[4 marks]

END OF QUESTIONS

A-level
Physics
Practice paper for AQA

Paper 3 – Section B (Astrophysics)

Time allowed: 2 hours

Materials

For this paper you must have:

- a pencil
- a ruler
- a calculator
- a data and formulae booklet
- a question paper/answer booklet for Section A.

Instructions

- Answer **all** questions.
- Show **all** your working.
- The total time for both sections of this section is 2 hours.

Information

- The maximum mark for this section is 35.

Name: ....

Section B

Answer **all** questions in this section.

| 0 1 | The glass lenses used in some optical refracting telescopes can suffer from chromatic aberration. |

0 1 · 1 Draw a diagram to show how light rays are affected by chromatic aberration in a lens.

[1 mark]

0 1 · 2 Suggest **one** way that chromatic aberration can be reduced or avoided in a refracting telescope.

[1 mark]

A 0.25 m diameter refracting telescope is used to observe the Moon. It has an objective lens with a focal length of 0.60 m. It is set up in normal adjustment and the angular magnification is ×20.

[0 1 · 3] Calculate how far apart the lenses are in normal adjustment.

[3 marks]

distance apart _____ m

[0 1 · 4] Calculate the angular resolution of the telescope (take $\lambda = 5 \times 10^{-7}$ m).

[2 marks]

angular resolution _____ unit _____

0 2   Reflecting telescopes are used to observe the Sun in both the radio wave and the X-ray regions of the electromagnetic spectrum.

0 2 · 1 State a suitable site for a radio telescope and an X-ray telescope. Explain why the site is suitable in each case.

[4 marks]

0 2 · 2 Compare features of these reflecting telescopes, explaining how the wavelength range affects the design.

[4 marks]

0 3 Rigel and Procyon are two stars visible from the Earth. **Table 1** gives some data for these stars.

Table 1

Star	Apparent magnitude	Absolute magnitude	Spectral class
Rigel	+0.12	−7.8	B
Procyon	+0.38	2.6	F

0 3 . 1 By considering the data deduce which star is closer to the Earth and explain your answer.

[2 marks]

0 3 . 2 Describe the spectrum of radiation received from each of the stars.

[4 marks]

Spectrum from Rigel:

Spectrum from Procyon:

The intensity of the radiation from a third star S is measured from a space telescope and plotted in **Figure 1**.

Figure 1

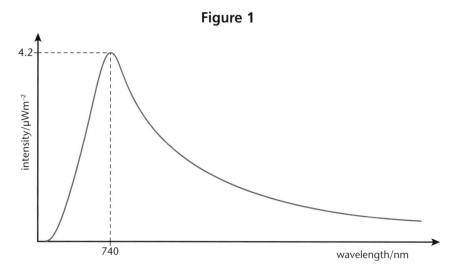

0 3 . 3 Show that the temperature of star S is about 4000 K.

[2 marks]

0 3 . 4 Star S is 6.5 ly from the Earth. Show that its power output is about 2 × 10²⁹ W and calculate the area of star S.

[4 marks]

area of star S _____ m²

| 0 4 | | Edwin Hubble made use of standard candles in his observations of galaxies.

| 0 4 | · | 1 | State what astronomers mean by a standard candle, and state an example.

[2 marks]

| 0 4 | · | 2 | Explain how Edwin Hubble determined the distances and velocities of galaxies and how he deduced that the Universe was expanding.

[6 marks]

END OF QUESTIONS

A-level
Physics
Practice paper for AQA

Paper 3 – Section B (Medical Physics)   Time allowed: 2 hours

Materials
For this paper you must have:
- a pencil
- a ruler
- a calculator
- a data and formulae booklet
- a question paper/answer book for Section A.

Instructions
- Answer **all** questions.
- Show **all** your working.
- The total time for both sections of this paper is 2 hours.

Information
- The maximum mark for this section is 35.

Name: ....

Section B

Answer **all** questions in this section.

---

0 1   A person who is short-sighted has an unaided far point 2.5 m from the eye.

0 1 . 1 State the type of lens required to correct a short-sighted eye.

[1 mark]

---

0 1 . 2 **Figure 1** is not to scale. The first two diagrams are for the unaided eye, the third diagram shows the eye with a corrective lens, which will give an aided far point at infinity. Complete the diagrams to show the path of the rays to the retina.

Assume the eye has a single refraction at the cornea.

Figure 1

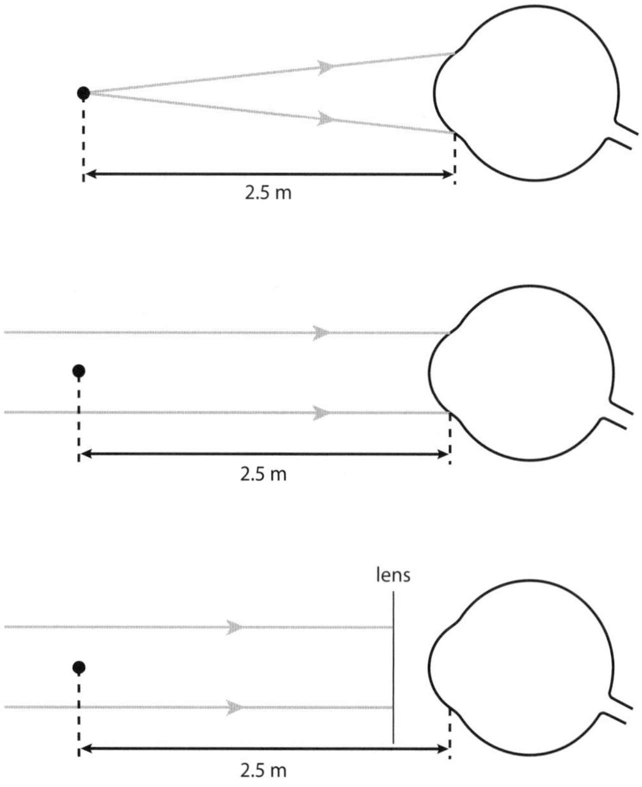

2.5 m

2.5 m

lens

2.5 m

[2 marks]

0 1 . 3 Calculate the power of the lens needed to correct the vision.

[3 marks]

power _____ D

0 1 . 4 An eye is astigmatic. Suggest a cause for this condition and describe the effect on the image produced by the eye.

[2 marks]

0 1 . 5 What type of lens is used to correct astigmatism?

[1 mark]

0 2   **Figure 2** shows an equal loudness curve for the normal human ear, at 0 phon.

Figure 2

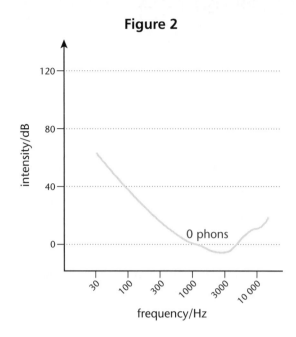

frequency/Hz

0 2 · 1 Explain what an equal loudness curve shows and state the significance of the 0 phon curve.

[2 marks]

_____

_____

_____

_____

0 2 · 2 Add to **Figure 2** an equal loudness curve for a person whose hearing has been permanently damaged by exposure to loud noise over a long period of time.

[3 marks]

0 2 · 3 Explain how this damaged hearing is different to that of an older person whose hearing has been affected by the normal aging process.

[3 marks]

0 2 · 4 A report states that listening to an MP3 player at an intensity level of 85 dB for extended times can cause hearing damage. Calculate the intensity, in W m^{-2}, of an 85 dB sound.

[3 marks]

intensity _____ W m^{-2}

0 3 Magnetic resonance (MR) scanners and X-ray CT (computed tomography) scanners are both used to produce visual images for medical diagnosis. Compare these techniques in terms of:
- patient safety
- convenience
- the information the images provide for doctors.

[6 marks]

0 4 Technetium-99m (Tc-99m) is a radioactive tracer used in nuclear medicine units in hospitals. It has a (physical) half-life of six hours. The Tc-99m is not delivered to hospitals. It is produced on site from a molybdenum-technetium generator by beta decay.

0 4 . 1 Explain why the Tc-99m is produced on site.

[1 mark]

....

....

0 4 . 2 Complete the nuclear equation for the production of Tc-99m from molybdenum.

[2 marks]

$$\boxed{}_{\boxed{}}\text{Mo} \rightarrow {}^{99}_{43}\text{Tc} + \boxed{}_{\boxed{}}\boxed{} + \bar{v}_e$$

0 4 . 3 Tc-99m is used for a bone scan. A dose of Tc-99m is injected into the patient's vein. State the nature of the radiation emitted and how it is detected.

[2 marks]

....

....

0 4 . 4 The biological half-life of Tc-99m is 15 hours. Calculate the effective half-life of Tc-99m.

[1 mark]

effective half-life _____ hours

0 4 . 5 A 740 MBq dose was injected into the patient. Calculate the activity of the Tc-99m remaining in the patient after 16 hours.

[3 marks]

activity _____ MBq

END OF QUESTIONS

Answers

Note: 'ecf.' stands for 'error carried forward'. If you get the wrong answer for part of a question and carry this mistake through to the next part of the question, 'allow ecf.' indicates that you can still get full marks if you do this part correctly.

Paper 1A

01.1 $K^- + p \rightarrow X + K^+$ **[1 mark]**

01.2 Charge: LHS (−1 e) + (+1 e) = 0 so
RHS = 0 = (charge on X) + (+1 e) so charge on X = (−1 e) **[1 mark]**

01.3 Baryon no.: LHS (0) + (1) = +1 so
RHS = +1 = (baryon no. of X) + (0) so
baryon no. of X = (+1) **[1 mark]**

Strangeness: LHS (−1) + (0) = −1 so
RHS = −1 = (strangeness of X) + (11)
so strangeness of X = (−2) **[1 mark]**

01.4 Baryon no. = 1 so 3 quarks **[1 mark]**
strangeness = −2 so 2 strange quarks, which have charge (−1/3 e) + (−1/3 e) = (−2/3 e) **[1 mark]** X has charge (−1 e) so third quark has charge (−1/3 e) so is a down quark **[1 mark]** **[dss scores 3 marks]**

02.1 Battery and ammeter in series **[1 mark]** and voltmeter in parallel with thermistor **[1 mark]**

02.2 Resistance: $1/R = 1/(200 + 100) + 1/(200 + 100) = 150\ \Omega$, $R = 150\ \Omega$ **[1 mark for series (200 + 100), 1 mark for parallel ($1/R = 1/R_1 + 1/R_2$ used with 300, 200 or 100), 1 mark for 150 Ω]**

Current: $I = (3\ V)/(150\ \Omega) = 0.020\ A = 20\ mA$ **[1 mark]**

02.3 Zero OR 0 A **[1 mark]** because there is no potential difference between A and B (because the potential difference between the battery and A and the battery and B is the same) **[1 mark]**.

02.4 Temperature increased **[1 mark]**, thermistor's resistance decreases as temperature increases so temperature increased **[1 mark]**.

02.5 Now lower resistance path through X than W **[1 mark]**, so more current through X than W **[1 mark]** (OR p.d. across X lower than across W so p.d. between A and B) so current in direction from A to B **[1 mark]**.

03.1 By conservation of momentum, momentum after collision = momentum before **[1 mark]** momentum before = (0.4 kg) × (0.30 m s⁻¹) + 0 = 0.12 kg m s⁻¹ = (0.4 kg + 0.25 kg) × v **[1 mark]** v = 0.18 m s⁻¹ **[1 mark, no marks for 0.2 as this is given in the question]**

03.2 Initial momentum = 0.12 kg m s⁻¹

final momentum (same mass and same speed but opposite direction) = −0.12 kg m s⁻¹

so change in momentum = 0.24 kg m s⁻¹ **[1 mark, allow calculation using speed of 0.18 gives 0.23 kg m s⁻¹ or speed of 0.2 gives 0.26 kg m s⁻¹, allow ecf. from 03.1]**

03.3 Elastic collision – kinetic energy is conserved; in inelastic collision – kinetic energy is not conserved **[1 mark, mark not awarded for 'energy is not conserved']**. Momentum is conserved in both elastic and inelastic collisions **[1 mark, must say both]**.

03.4 Momentum before = (0.2 kg) × (0.30 m s⁻¹) + (0.2 kg) × (−0.20 m s⁻¹) **[1 mark]** = (0.060 − 0.040) = (0.020 kg m s⁻¹). By conservation of momentum, momentum after collision = momentum before, momentum after = (0.2 kg) × v + (0.2 kg) × (0.30 m s⁻¹) **[1 mark]** 0.020 = 0.2 v + 0.060 so 0.2 v = −0.040 so v = 0.2 m s⁻¹ **[1 mark]**

E_K before = ½ (0.2)(0.30)² + ½ (0.2)(−0.20)² = 0.009 + 0.004 = 0.013 J

E_K after = ½ (0.2)(0.30)² + ½ (0.2)(−0.20)² = 0.009 + 0.004 = 0.013 J **[1 mark for E_K 'before' or 'after']**

E_K before = E_K after **[1 mark for showing this]** so elastic **[no mark for just writing this, i.e. guessing]**

04.1 $F = k\ \Delta L$ $k = mg/\Delta L = (0.31 × 9.81)/(0.14)$ **[1 mark]**

k = 21.7 N m⁻¹ (or 22 N m⁻¹ (2 s.f.)) **[1 mark]**

04.2 $T = 2\pi\sqrt{\dfrac{m}{k}} = 2\pi\sqrt{\dfrac{0.31}{22}} = 0.75\ s$ **[1 mark, allow using k = 20 N m⁻¹ gives 0.78 s]**

04.3 Maximum tension will occur when the extension is the greatest value **[1 mark]**. This is when the mass is at the lowest point **[1 mark, OR when extension = 0.14 m + 0.025 m = 0.165 m]**.

$F = k\,\Delta l = 22 \times 0.165 = 3.6$ N **[1 mark]**
(OR $20 \times 0.165 = 3.3$ N)

04.4 Both m and k are constants **[1 mark]** so the period will not change **[1 mark]**. The initial extension will be less, hence the maximum tension will decrease because g is less on the Moon **[1 mark]**.

05.1 Loss of E_p between **X** and **Y** = gain in E_K at **Y**
$mg\Delta h = \frac{1}{2}mv^2$ (9.81 m s^{-2})(0.40 m) $= \frac{1}{2}v^2$
[1 mark]

$v = \sqrt{(2 \times 9.81 \times 0.40)}$ m s^{-1} = 2.8 m s^{-1} **[1 mark]**

05.2 Loss in E_K between **Y** and **Z** = gain in E_p between **Y** and **Z** so overall loss in E_p between **X** and **Z** = E_K at **Z** Δh = 0.30 m $mg\Delta h = \frac{1}{2}mv^2$ (9.81 m s^{-2})(0.30 m) $= \frac{1}{2}v^2$ **[1 mark]**

$v = \sqrt{(2 \times 9.81 \times 0.30)}$ m s^{-1} = 2.4 m s^{-1} **[1 mark]**

OR using value from 5.1 **[allow incorrect value]**: loss in E_K between **Y** and **Z** = gain in E_p at **Z** Δh = 0.10 m $mg\Delta h = \frac{1}{2}mv_Y^2 - \frac{1}{2}mv_z^2$ (9.81 m s^{-2})(0.10 m) $= \frac{1}{2}(2.80)^2 - \frac{1}{2}v^2$ **[1 mark]**

$v = \sqrt{((2.80)^2 - 2 \times 9.81 \times 0.10)}$ m s^{-1} = 2.4 m s^{-1} **[1 mark]**

05.3

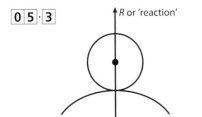

R or 'reaction'

mg or W or 'weight'

[1 mark]

$mg - R = \dfrac{mv^2}{r}$ **[1 mark]**

$(0.006 \text{ kg})(9.81 \text{ m s}^{-2}) - R = \dfrac{(0.006 \text{ kg})(2.43 \text{ m s}^{-1})^2}{(0.75 \text{ m})}$

[1 mark, allow incorrect v from 1.2]

$R = 0.012$ N **[1 mark]**

06.1 Infrared **[1 mark]**

06.2 $f = c/\lambda$ $f = (3 \times 10^8$ m s$^{-1})/(660 \times 10^{-9}$ m$)$

$= 4.5 \times 10^{14}$ Hz **[1 mark]**

$E = hf$ $E = (6.63 \times 10^{-34}$ Js$) \times (4.5 \times 10^{14}$ Hz$)$
[1 mark] $= 3.0 \times 10^{-19}$ J (allow 2.98×10^{-19} J to 3.01×10^{-19} J)

In eV: $E = (3.0 \times 10^{-19}$ J$)/(1.6 \times 10^{-19}$ C$) = 1.9$ eV
[1 mark]

06.3 Blue light is absorbed by an electron which moves to a higher energy level **[1 mark]**. The electron then drops to a lower energy level emitting a photon of longer wavelength/ lower energy in the yellow part of the spectrum **[1 mark]**.

06.4 No **[0 marks for this, marks are for explanation]** because the red photon has less energy than the green and blue photons **[1 mark]** and cannot excite the electron to a high enough energy level for it to drop down emitting green light or blue light **[1 mark, allow explanation using a calculation showing energy of green or blue photon and comparing with energy of red photon]**.

06.5 $\sin\theta = n\lambda/d = 1 \times (450 \times 10^{-9}$ m$)/(1 \times 10^{-3}$ m/1500$)$ **[1 mark]** $\theta = 42°$ **[1 mark]**

06.6 White light straight through and on either side a blue line and a yellow line **[1 mark]**. The blue line is closest to the straight-through position **[1 mark, allow a labelled diagram]**.

Paper 1B

07 C: $^{204}_{82}$Pb + $^{4}_{2}$He $\rightarrow$ $^{208}_{83}$Bi + $^{0}_{1}$e **[1 mark]**

08 B: $\eta = \dfrac{F}{6\pi r v}$ units: $\dfrac{\text{N}}{\text{(m)(m s}^{-1})} = \dfrac{\text{kg m}}{\text{s}^2} \times \dfrac{\text{s}}{\text{m}^2} = \dfrac{\text{kg}}{\text{s m}} =$ kg m^{-1} s^{-1} **[1 mark]**

09 C: Energy of photon, which depends on its frequency = work function of metal + max. kinetic energy of electron (which $= \frac{1}{2}mv^2$) **[1 mark]**

10 C: λ_B has the greatest energy **[1 mark]**. Since $E = hf = \dfrac{hc}{\lambda}$ it must also have the highest frequency. λ_A is the longest wavelength and λ_B is the shortest wavelength. The length of the lines on the diagram are proportional to energy and frequency, not wavelength.

11 B: $V \propto d^3$, % error in V = 3 × % error in d because d is cubed when calculating V **[1 mark]**

12 **B:** Note that positron is the same size mass and charge as electron (only sign is different) so either look up Q/m for electron and proton in data booklet and calculate alpha (roughly) from $(2 \times 1.6 \times 10^{-19}/4 \times 1.67 \times 10^{27}) = 4.8 \times 10^7$ OR use electron mass = 1/2000 × proton mass and alpha particle mass = 4 × proton mass together with electron charge = proton charge and alpha particle charge = 2 × proton charge to get the ratio positron : proton : alpha particle = 2000 : 1 : 0.5 **[1 mark]**.

13 **A:** Use $f = \dfrac{1}{2l}\sqrt{\dfrac{T}{\mu}}$, $f \propto \sqrt{T}$, when T changed to $2T$, f changed to $\sqrt{2}f = \sqrt{2} \times 200$ Hz **[1 mark]**

14 **D:** Use $R = \dfrac{\rho l}{A} = \dfrac{\rho l}{\pi d^2/4} = \dfrac{\rho l_2}{d^2}$ so length $l_2 = \dfrac{4l}{\pi}$ **[1 mark]**

15 **D:** As the third filter is rotated from 0° some light is transmitted through it except at 0° and multiples of 90°; some of this light is then transmitted through the final filter except (again) at 0° and multiples of 90° **[1 mark]**.

16 **D:** $\sin\theta_c = n_{\text{cladding}}/n_{\text{core}}$ and $n_{\text{cladding}} = c/c_{\text{cladding}}$ and $n_{\text{core}} = c/c_{\text{core}}$ so $\sin\theta_c = c_{\text{core}}/c_{\text{cladding}} = (2.02 \times 10^8)/(2.08 \times 10^8) = 0.971$ $\theta_c = 76°$ **[1 mark]**

17 **C:** Width of fringes $w = \lambda D/s$ frequency is ×½ so wavelength will be × 2 ($c = f\lambda$) so w will be × 2 **[1 mark]**

18 **C:** Taking moments about the centre of the beam – so that its weight has no effect. $40 \times F = 20 \times T$ so $T:F = 40:20 = 2:1$ **[1 mark]**

19 **A:** A and B have anticlockwise moment, total = 2 × 10 × radius = 20 × radius. For equilibrium C has clockwise moment 20 × radius **[1 mark]**

20 **D:** Motion at 90° is independent. East: $a = F/m = (0.2)/(0.5) = 0.4$ m s^{-2} $v = u + at = 0 + (0.4)(10) = 4$ m s^{-1}. Resultant velocity of 3 m s^{-1} S + 4 m s^{-1} E cannot be East (or = $\tan^{-1} 4/3 = 53°$ East of South) magnitude using Pythagoras = $\sqrt{3^2 + 4^2}$ = 5 m s^{-1} **[1 mark]**

21 **C:** For one spring $k = F/\Delta L$. In series both springs extend so the extension is doubled, $k_s = F/2\Delta L$ $\left(\text{or use} \dfrac{1}{k_s} = \dfrac{1}{k} + \dfrac{1}{k} = \dfrac{2}{k},\right) = k_s = \dfrac{k}{2}$, in parallel each spring supports half the load, so extension is halved $k_p = F/0.5x$ (or use $k_p = k + k = 2k$) so $k_p = 2k$ **[1 mark]**

22 **D:** Both will fall with vertical acceleration g. Both will have constant horizontal velocity **[1 mark]**.

23 **C:** Time of flight for P should be twice time to greatest height, so vertically $u = v\sin\theta$ and $v = 0$ and $t_p = \dfrac{2v}{g}\sin\theta$; for Q $t_q = \dfrac{2v}{g}\sin(90-\theta) = \dfrac{2v}{g}\cos\theta$.

Dividing two equations gives $\dfrac{t_p}{t_q} = \dfrac{\frac{2v}{g}\sin\theta}{\frac{2v}{g}\cos\theta} = \tan\theta$

so $t_q = \dfrac{t_p}{\tan\theta}$ OR use time of flight is time for vertical distance to reach 0. Use $s = ut + \dfrac{1}{2}at^2$ with $s = 0$ $g = -9.81$ gives $ut = \dfrac{1}{2}(9.81)t^2$ so $u = \dfrac{1}{2}(9.81)t$.

For P: $v\sin\theta = \dfrac{1}{2}(9.81)t_p$. For Q: (use $\sin\theta =$ cos (90°– θ)) $v\cos\theta = \dfrac{1}{2}(9.81)t_q$. Dividing two equations

gives $\dfrac{v\cos\theta}{v\sin\theta} = \dfrac{\frac{1}{2}(9.81)t_q}{\frac{1}{2}(9.81)t_p} = \dfrac{t_q}{t_p} = \dfrac{1}{\tan\theta}$ so $t_q = \dfrac{t_p}{\tan\theta}$ **[1 mark]**

24 **A:** Reaction force is greater when the lift is either accelerating upwards (speeding up) or decelerating downwards (slowing down). Reaction force is only less when the lift is accelerating downwards (speeding up) or decelerating upwards (slowing down) **[1 mark]**.

25 **C:** On a frictionless ramp, the work done is only against the weight of the crate. The work done is Mgh in both cases (and equal to the increase in potential energy) **[1 mark]**.

26 **B:** Power is mgh/t, X: (30 g × 120)/(2 × 60) = 30 g, Y: (8 g × 6)/(1.5) = 32 g, Z: (4 g × 15)/(10) = 6 g **[1 mark]**

27 **A:** Use $\varepsilon = I(R + r)$ $\varepsilon = V + Ir$ $9.0 = 7.8 + 1.5r$ $r = 1.2/1.5 = 0.8$ Ω **[1 mark]**

28 **D:** Use potential divider equations; the ratio of p.d.s V_1/V_2 is the same as the ratio of resistances R_1/R_2 and $V_1 + V_2$ = constant. As it gets darker resistance of LDR R_2 increases so V_2 increases. Similarly, when R_1 is increased V_1 increases and V_2 decreases, which has the effect that it must get darker (so that R_2 increases more before the light switches on) **[1 mark]**.

29 **D:** The question is about the total energy, which does not change. If it was potential energy, B and C would be correct and if it was kinetic energy A would be correct **[1 mark]**.

3 0 **B:** Because it is a friction force it opposes motion and is always opposite to the velocity **[1 mark]**.

3 1 **D:** Vertical component of reaction

$R\cos\theta = mg$ horizontal component $R\sin\theta = \dfrac{mv^2}{r}$

(the centripetal force on m) dividing the two

equations $\tan\theta = \dfrac{\dfrac{mv^2}{r}}{mg} = \dfrac{v^2}{rg}$ **[1 mark]**

Paper 2A

0 1 · 1 $Q = mc\Delta\theta = (mc\Delta\theta)_{PCM} + (mc\Delta\theta)_{container}$
= 0.4 × 2200 × (37 − 15) + 0.24 × 840 (37 − 15)

[1 mark]

= 19360 + 4435
= 23800 J **[1 mark]**

0 1 · 2 $E = IVt = 1.7 × 12 × 90 × 60 = 110160$ J **[1 mark]**

States or shows that electrical energy transferred = thermal energy transferred to raise temperature of solid PCM and container to 37 °C, to then raise temperature of PCM and glass container from 37 °C to 39 °C and to melt the PCM **[1 mark]**.

$Q = 23800 + (0.4 × 2600 × (39 − 37)) + (0.24 × 840 (39 − 37)) + (0.4)L$ **[1 mark]**

$110160 = 23800 + 0.4L + 2080 + 403.2$, $0.4L$
= 83876.8, $L = 210000$ J kg^{-1} **[1 mark]**

0 1 · 3 If the body temperature goes above 37 °C, energy is transferred to the PCM to melt it and if the body temperature falls below 37 °C, energy is transferred from the PCM to warm the body **[1 mark]**.

0 2 · 1 1. Empirical means observed from the results of experiment OR the gas laws are based on observations from experiments **[1 mark]**. (They predict results but don't explain why.)

2. Kinetic theory is based on assumptions leading to deductions using other knowledge and theories **[1 mark, allow any equivalent statements]**.

0 2 · 2 Density **[1 mark]**. N = number of molecules, m = molecular mass, V = volume of gas, Nm = total mass, Nm/V = mass/volume = density **[1 mark]**

0 2 · 3 $[(v_1)^2 + (v_2)^2 + (v_3)^2 + (v_4)^2] \div 4$ **[1 mark]**

0 2 · 4 Use $\dfrac{1}{2}m(c_{rms})^2 = \dfrac{3}{2}kT$ (OR $= \dfrac{3\,RT}{2N_A}$) m

= 0.028/(6.02 × 10²³) kg **[1 mark]**

$T = \dfrac{m(c_{rms})^2}{3k}$

$= \dfrac{0.028 × 520^2}{3 × 6.02 × 10^{23} × 1.38 × 10^{-23}}$ **[1 mark]**

= 304 K **[1 mark]**

0 3 · 1 $F_G = \dfrac{Gm_1m_2}{r^2}$

$= \dfrac{(6.7 × 10^{-11})(9.11 × 10^{-31})(1.67 × 10^{-27})}{(5.3 × 10^{-11})^2}$

= 3.6 × 10⁻⁴⁷ N **[1 mark]**

$F_E = \dfrac{1}{4\pi\epsilon_0}\dfrac{Q_1Q_2}{r^2} = \dfrac{1}{4\pi(8.85 × 10^{-12})}\dfrac{(1.6 × 10^{-19})^2}{(5.3 × 10^{-11})^2}$

= 8.2 × 10⁻⁸ N **[1 mark]**

Ratio: F_E/F_G = 8.2 × 10⁻⁸ N/3.6 × 10⁻⁴⁷
N = 2.3 × 10³⁹ **[1 mark, no units]**

The gravitational force between a proton and an electron is of the order of 10³⁹ times smaller than the electrostatic force, so is negligible and can be ignored when calculating the forces on subatomic particles **[1 mark]**.

0 3 · 2 **[Must give both statements for each mark]**
Differences: 1. Gravity is always attractive, electrostatic is attractive or repulsive. 2. Gravity acts on all matter (objects with mass), electrostatic acts only on charged matter (charged objects). 3. You can shield objects from electrostatic forces, but not from gravitational forces. 4. Permittivity for electric fields depends on the medium in which the field exists, but for gravitational fields there is no difference in any material. 5. Gravitational field always directed towards mass producing it, electric is towards a negative charge but away from a positive charge. 6. Mass of 1 kg produces a small field, 1 C produces a very strong field. 7. Gravitational potential is always negative, but electric potential is negative for negative charges and positive for positive charges.

Similarities: 1. In a radial field force varies as inverse square of the distance between objects. 2. Force between two objects proportional to the product of both (charges for electrostatic, masses for gravitational). 3. The field strength in a radial field is proportional to the mass/charge producing it. 4. Spherical and point objects have a radial field. 5. Work done in moving a mass or charge across a potential difference is calculated by multiplying the mass/charge by the potential difference. 6. Both types of potential are proportional to $1/r$ in a radial field. 7. In a uniform field the potential is proportional to the distance. 8. In a uniform field the field has the same magnitude and direction at all points. **[5 marks: 1 mark for a difference, 1 mark for a similarity, 3 marks for additional similarities or differences]**

04·1 The changing electric current in the coils produces a changing magnetic field so there is changing magnetic flux through the sheet **[1 mark]**. The changing magnetic flux induces emfs in the copper sheet **[1 mark]**. The emfs produce currents in the sheet **[1 mark]** and this has a heating effect due to the resistance of the sheet **[1 mark]**.

04·2 **[Either order]** 1. Increase the frequency of the alternating current. The induced emf is proportional to the rate of change of flux linkage, so by increasing the frequency of the alternating current the induced emf will be increased **[1 mark]**. 2. Increase the current in the coils, which will increase the magnetic field, increasing the maximum flux so that the rate of change of flux linkage is larger **[1 mark]**.

04·3 The emfs induced will be unchanged, but the currents will be reduced **[1 mark]**, although resistance is increased. (Thermal energy transfer = V^2/R.) Net effect will be a decrease in the rate of heating due to reduced current **[1 mark]**.

05·1 $E = V/d = 10 \times 10^3/0.02 = 5.0 \times 10^5$ **[1 mark]**
$F = EQ = 5.0 \times 10^5 \times 1.6 \times 10^{-19} = 8.0 \times 10^{-14}$ N **[1 mark]**

05·2 $F = ma$ $a = 8.0 \times 10^{-14}$ N$/1.67 \times 10^{-27}$ kg **[1 mark]**
$= 4.8 \times 10^{13}$ m s^{-2} $v^2 = u^2 + 2as = 0 + (2 \times 4.8 \times 10^{13} \times 0.01)$ **[1 mark, allow ecf. for a]** $v = 9.8 \times 10^5$ m s^{-1} **[1 mark for correct evaluation of both to more than 1 s.f.]**

05·3 Use of $v^2 = u^2 + 2as$ $(3 \times 10^7)^2 = (9.8 \times 10^5)^2 + (2 \times 4.8 \times 10^{13})$ $(2n \times 0.02)$ **[1 mark for attempt to use with speed acceleration and distance, 1 mark for correct use]**

Gives $n = 234.1$ so 235 laps needed **[1 mark, allow ecf. for own values calculated in 05.2, allow use of values given in 05.2]**

05·4 Proton marked on track with direction of motion tangent to track in direction from source to target. Force at right angles to track, directly towards source **[1 mark]**. Magnetic field is vertically upwards (left-hand rule) so north pole is below the Ds, south pole above **[1 mark]**.

05·5 F is at 90° to B so $F = Bev$ AND $F = mv^2/r$ **[1 mark]**
$Bev = mv^2/r$ **[1 mark]**

05·6 So that the protons do not collide with air molecules and be stopped or deflected **[1 mark]**

06·1 Mass defect $= 238.04955 - (234.043924 + 4.00151) = 4.116 \times 10^{-3}$ u **[1 mark]**

$E = mc^2$

Energy $= 4.116 \times 10^{-3}$ u $\times 1.661 \times 10^{-27}$ kg $\times (3 \times 10^8)^2$ (m s$^{-1})^2$ OR $= 4.116 \times 10^{-3}$ u $\times 931.5$ MeV $\times 1.6 \times 10^{-13}$ (J per MeV) **[1 mark]**
$= 6.2 \times 10^{-13}$ J **[1 mark, allow 1 u = 931.3 MeV]**

06·2 238 g of Pu238 contains 6.02×10^{23} atoms
4300 g contains $4300/238 \times 6.02 \times 10^{23}$ **[1 mark]** $= 1.1 \times 10^{25}$

06·3 Half-life = 88 years
$\lambda = (\ln 2)/T_{1/2} = (\ln 2)/(88 \times 365 \times 24 \times 60 \times 60)$
$= 2.50 \times 10^{-10}$ s^{-1} **[1 mark]**

$A = \lambda N = 2.50 \times 10^{-10} \times 1.1 \times 10^{25}$
$= 2.75 \times 10^{15}$ Bq **[1 mark]**

OR $\lambda = 7.88 \times 10^{-3}$ y^{-1} $A = \lambda N = 7.88 \times 10^{-3}$ y^{-1} $\times 1.1 \times 10^{25}/(365 \times 24 \times 60 \times 60)$ **[allow $N = 1 \times 10^{25}$ or ecf. from 06.2]**

06·4 Total energy = energy per decay × number of decays

Power = energy per second = energy per decay × number of decays per second

Power $= 6.2 \times 10^{-13}$ J **[allow ecf. from 06.1]** $\times 2.75 \times 10^{15}$ Bq **[allow ecf. from 06.3]** = 1705 W **[1 mark]**

06·5 Deep-space probes are far from the Sun and little solar energy is available. Dust storms on Mars can cover panels. During the night or when probes are behind planets they will not receive radiation **[1 mark for two points made]**.

So batteries will not charge and electronics will shut down. RTGs provide a continuous supply that will not be interrupted **[1 mark for a suitable explanation]**.

06·6 $F = m_1 r \omega^2 = Gm_1 m_2 / r^2$ **[1 mark]** $r^3 = Gm_2/\omega^2$

$1/\omega^2 = r^3/Gm_2$

Use of $\omega = 2\pi f$ and $f = 1/T$ (or $T = 2\pi/\omega$) **[1 mark]** $T^2 = 4\pi^2 (1/\omega^2)$

$T^2 = 4\pi^2 (r^3/Gm_2)$

$T^2 = (4\pi^2/Gm_2) r^3$ AND π, G and m_2 are constants **[1 mark]** so $T^2 \propto r^3$

06·7 $T_{Earth} = 365$ days $T_{Mars} = 687$ days. Use

$$\frac{T_M^2}{T_E^2} = \frac{\left(\dfrac{4\pi^2}{Gm_2}\right) r_M^3}{\left(\dfrac{4\pi^2}{Gm_2}\right) r_E^3} = \frac{r_M^3}{r_E^3}$$

$$\frac{T_M^2}{T_E^2} = \frac{687^2}{365^2} = \frac{r_M^3}{r_E^3}$$ **[1 mark]**

ratio $\dfrac{r_M}{r_E} = \left(\dfrac{687}{365}\right)^{\frac{2}{3}} = 1.52$ **[1 mark]** ...

radius $r_M = 1.52 \times (1.50 \times 10^{11})$ m $= 2.3 \times 10^{11}$ m **[1 mark]**

Paper 2B

07 **C:** $p_1/T_1 = p_2/T_2$ when the temperature is the absolute temperature in kelvin **[1 mark]**

$$\frac{p}{(T + 273)} = \frac{2p}{(T_{new} + 273)}$$ when T and T_{new} are in °C. Rearranging: $(T_{new} + 273) = 2(T + 273)$ so $T_{new} = 2T + 273$

08 **C:** The internal energy of a system is the sum of the average kinetic energies and the potential energies of the atoms. For an ideal gas the potential energy is zero **[1 mark]**.

09 **D:** $F = GmM/r^2$ so $F \propto \dfrac{1}{r^2}$ **[1 mark]**

10 **C:** The work done in moving a unit mass from infinity to that point **[1 mark]**.

11 **A:** $V_{Earth} = -GM/R = 6.3 \times 10^7$ J kg^{-1} $V_{Jupiter} = -G(320M)/(11R) = (320/11)(-GM/R) = (29.09)$ $(-6.3 \times 10^7$ J kg$^{-1}) = -1.8 \times 10^9$ J kg^{-1} **[1 mark]**

12 **C:** $V = -G(3M)/(3r) = -GM/r$ The total potential is the sum of the potential at X due to both masses $= -GM/r + (-G(10M)/(5r)) = -GM/r - 2GM/r = -3GM/r = 3V$ **[1 mark]**

13 **C:** Geosynchronus and geostationary orbits both have a period of 24 hours, and will be overhead at each point in the orbit once a day. Geostationary is the special orbit that follows the equator (in the equatorial plane) and so is overhead at all times **[1 mark]**.

14 **D:** $F = -(Q)(-4Q)/d^2 = 4Q^2/d^2$ $F_{new} = -(2Q)(-3Q)/(d/2)^2 = 6Q^2/(d^2/4) = 24Q^2/d^2 = 6F$ **[1 mark]**

15 **B:** $\frac{1}{2} mv^2 = eV$ so $v \propto \sqrt{V}$ **[1 mark]**

16 **B:** Work done moving X to Y: Field is uniform so X and Z are at 250 V and Y at 150 V. Difference = 100 V (or $E = 500$ V/50 mm $= 10$ V mm^{-1} and XY = 10 mm gives 100 V). Work done $= QV = (1.6 \times 10^{-19})(100) = 1.6 \times 10^{-17}$ J, X to Z is along an equipotential surface (250 V) so work done = 0 **[1 mark]**

17 **C:** From $C = \dfrac{A\varepsilon_0 \varepsilon_r}{d}$ using a dielectric with relative permittivity $\varepsilon_r = 2$ will double the capacitance to $C_{new} = 2C$. $Q_{new} = (2C)V = 2Q$ and $E_{new} = \frac{1}{2}(2Q)V = 2E$ **[1 mark]**

18 **D:** $V = V_0 e^{\frac{-t}{RC}}$ to get an expression in the form $y = mx + c$ where $y = V$ and $x = t$. Take logs of both sides: $\ln V = \ln V_0 - \dfrac{t}{RC} = -\left(\dfrac{1}{RC}\right)t + \ln V_0$ so $y = \ln V$ and $x = t$ **[1 mark]**

19 **B:** $\tau = RC$ so τ is the time for the charge to fall to $1/e$ times the initial value. After 47 s the charge will be $\left(\dfrac{1}{e} \times 10\mu C\right) = 3.68\mu C \sim 3.7\mu C$ **[1 mark]**

20 **B:** Use an equation containing flux density B. $F = BIl$ is good as I and l are base units already. LHS = N = kg m s^{-2} RHS = (units of B) (A) (m) so units of B = kg m s^{-2} A^{-1} m^{-1} = kg A^{-1} s^{-2} **[1 mark]**

21 **A:** flux linkage $N\Phi = BAN\cos\theta$

$A = l^2 \cos\theta = 1$ so $N\Phi = Bl^2 N$ new flux linkage $= B\left(\dfrac{l}{2}\right)^2 (2N) = \dfrac{1}{2}Bl^2 N$

$= \frac{1}{2}$ original flux linkage **[1 mark]**

22 **D:** emf $\varepsilon = \Delta\Phi/\Delta t$ so $\Delta\Phi/\Delta t = \Delta(BA)/\Delta t = B\Delta A/\Delta t$ the change in area is the area swept out by the wing in a time that depends on its speed so $\Delta A/\Delta t = 25 \times 125 = 3125$ m^2 s^{-1} $\varepsilon = 5.0 \times 10^{-5} \times 3125 = 0.156$ V $= 0.16$ V (2 s.f.) **[1 mark]**

23 **D:** Remember: the rms value is related to the peak value, and will be less than the peak value **[1 mark]**

24 **D:** Changing the number of turns changes the output voltage. Improving the insulation will increase the running temperature so the resistance of the coils increases – leading to increased energy transfer as heat. An iron core made of layers will reduce eddy currents, and reduce energy transfers to the core **[1 mark]**.

25 **C:** The Rutherford model is that the atom has a small central nucleus of high density **[1 mark]**.

26 **A:** Using $\lambda_X = \dfrac{\ln 2}{T_{1/2}}$ and $A = \lambda_X N$ for X. For Y

$$\lambda_Y = \frac{\ln 2}{3T_{1/2}} = \frac{\lambda_X}{3} \text{ and } A_Y = \lambda_Y 2N = \frac{\lambda_X}{3} 2N = \frac{2}{3} A$$

[1 mark]

27 **A:** Background radiation arises from cosmic ray interactions from space, from naturally occurring radiation from rocks, and a small amount of man-made radiation. The cosmic microwave background is microwave radiation (non-ionising) **[1 mark]**.

28 **B:** Fraction remaining is
$$\frac{N}{N_0} = e^{-\lambda t} = e^{-(1.13 \times 10^{-3} \times 15 \times 60)} = 0.36,$$
as a percentage = 36% **[1 mark]**

29 **C:** From the equation for the radius, $R \propto A^{\frac{1}{3}}$ so volume $V = \frac{4}{3}\pi R^3 \propto R^3 \propto A$. Density $= M/V$ and as mass and volume are both proportional to A, density is independent of A **[1 mark]**.

30 **D:** Think of the binding energy per nucleon curve. Fe-56 is the most stable and has the greatest binding energy per nucleon. Light nuclides (less than iron) can fuse by increasing their BE per nucleon – the product is closer to Fe-56. Heavy nuclides can fission by increasing their BE per nucleon to give to lighter nuclides – products closer to Fe-56 **[1 mark]**.

31 **C:** Moderator is to slow neutrons, so high number of interactions required. Control rods are to reduce reaction when fully used so must reduce neutrons and do this by absorbing neutrons. Coolant is required to transfer energy so a high specific heat capacity leads to large energy transfer with small change in temperature **[1 mark]**.

Paper 3A

01·1 Precautions: Wear eye protection. Check the breaking strength of the wire and ensure it is not exceeded. Explanation: If the wire breaks the potential energy transferred may make the end of the wire whiplash.

Precaution: If heavy masses are being used ensure they can fall safely, e.g. into a bucket. Explanation: so they don't damage floor/feet. **[3 marks: 1 mark for each safety precaution, 1 mark for an explanation of one of the precautions stated]**

01·2 A micrometer **[1 mark]**

01·3 Diameter = (0.77 + 0.77 + 0.79)/3 mm = 0.777 ± (0.79 – 0.77)/2 = 0.01 so value (with appropriate s.f.) = 0.78(± 0.01) mm **[2 marks: 1 mark for mean value, 1 mark for uncertainty]**

01·4 Cross-sectional area = $\pi d^2/4 = \pi (0.78 \times 10^{-3})^2/4 = 4.78 \times 10^{-7}$ m² **[1 mark]** % uncertainty = 2 × % uncertainty in d = 2 × (0.01/0.78) × 100 **[1 mark, ecf. for uncertainty in d]** = 2.56% = 3% **[1 mark]**

01·5 Tension in wire OR mass hung on wire; original length of wire; extended length of wire (not extension, unless indicated how this is to be measured directly, rather than calculated); diameter of cross-section (not area). **[3 marks for all four points made, 2 marks for three points made, 1 mark for two points made, 0 marks for one point made.]** Note that area is incorrect as it cannot be measured directly.

01·6 Attempt to calculate a gradient from a large triangle, using at least half of the line **[1 mark]**

Gradient = $\Delta y/\Delta x$ with a pair of correct values from the graph **[1 mark]**

Young modulus = 1.8×10^{11} Pa (or correct equivalent, e.g. 180 GPa) **[1 mark, answers that round to 180 GPa are acceptable]**

02·1 So that the pendulum swings with SHM and equation can be used **[1 mark]**

02·2 More readings **[1 mark]** OR smaller intervals between lengths **[1 mark]** / larger range of lengths **[1 mark]**. More accurate measurement of length **[1 mark]**. All times measured to same higher precision **[1 mark]**. Repeats and mean of values taken **[1 mark]**.

02·3 Time from the centre of the swing **[1 mark]**. Use a fiducial mark **[allow description of this, 1 mark]**.

02·4 $T = 2\pi \sqrt{l/g}$, $T^2 = 4\pi^2 (l/g)$, $T^2 = (4\pi^2/g)$ compare with straight line $y = mx + c$ shows graph will be straight line with gradient $m = (4\pi^2/g)$ **[1 mark]** and intercept $c = 0$ **[1 mark]**, i.e. through origin $(4\pi^2/g) = 4.2$ $g = 4\pi^2/4.2 = 9.4$ m s⁻² **[1 mark]**

02.5 Uncertainty ± 3 mm **[1 mark]** uncertainty using metre rule = 0.5 mm at each end = 1 mm add to uncertainty in x = 3 mm **[1 mark]**

02.6 Systematic error **[1 mark]**

02.7 The line does not go through the origin **[1 mark]** (straight line of same gradient). Value of g is unchanged **[1 mark]** (because gradient unchanged) **[allow explanation that if the line is forced through the origin the gradient will be shallower so the value of g will be increased (because $g = 4\pi^2/\text{gradient}$)].**

03.1 Safety precaution, **any one from**: wear eye protection OR use a plastic tube, not glass OR stand clear of the tube when using the pump or similar suggestion.

Explanation: because the high pressure may rupture the tube or cause the equipment to come apart suddenly **[2 marks: 1 mark for one safety precaution, 1 mark for explanation].**

03.2 To keep temperature constant OR to let temperature return to room temperature **[1 mark]**

03.3 Read at eye level OR use a no parallax method **[1 mark]**

03.4 Column heading for 1/V with unit as shown below **[1 mark]**, calculations correct as shown below **[1 mark]** to 2 s.f. **[1 mark]**

Pressure p/x 10^5 Pa	Volume V/cm³	1/volume $1/V$/cm⁻³
1.0	40.0	0.025
1.4	29.0	0.034
1.8	22.0	0.045
2.2	18.0	0.056
2.5	16.0	0.063
3.0	13.0	0.077

03.5 Vertical axis labelled: 1/Volume $1/V$ cm⁻³ **[1 mark]**. Correct plotting to 0.5 square **[1 mark]**. Best-fit line by eye **[1 mark]**

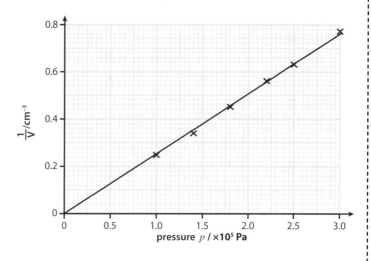

03.6 Appropriate comment **[1 mark]**, e.g. If the graph is a straight line: this shows that the pressure is proportional to $1/V$, i.e. inversely proportional to V and the gas obeys Boyle's law.

[ecf.: If incorrectly plotted the line does not give a straight line and so a mark would be awarded for saying that the pressure is not proportional to $1/V$, i.e. not inversely proportional to V and the gas does not obey Boyle's law]

03.7 **Any 4 marks:** Description/labelled diagram of closed glass capillary tube containing gas (air) V, sealed with 'bead' of sulphuric acid and a scale behind to measure V **[1 mark]** in a water bath with thermometer to measure temperature **[1 mark]**. Heat water and measure temperature and volume **[1 mark]**. Wear safety goggles **[1 mark]**. Plot values of volume against kelvin temperature **[1 mark]**. Charles' law is shown by a straight line through zero volume at 0 K **[allow 0 volume at –273 °C, 1 mark, allow a workable safe alternative experiment to measure V and T].**

Paper 3B (Astrophysics)

01.1

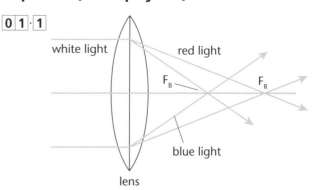

Colours (or correct f or λ) labelled, rays focused, blue/violet focal point closer to lens than red **[1 mark]**

0 1 . 2 **Any one from:** view monochromatic light (filter). Use lenses made with glass of different refractive index [allow use very long telescope, 1 mark for one suggestion]

0 1 . 3 $M = f_o/f_e$ $20 = 0.60/f_e$ [1 mark] $f_e = 0.030$ m [1 mark] distance apart $= f_o + f_e = 0.60 + 0.030 = 0.63$ m [1 mark]

0 1 . 4 θ in radians $\approx \lambda/D$. For λ use 5×10^{-7} m as light from the Moon, (same as Sun) so use middle of visible spectrum. D is diameter of lens $= 0.25$ m. $\theta = 5 \times 10^{-7}/0.25 = 2 \times 10^{-6}$ rad [1 mark] use of formula with 5×10^{-7} m value for wavelength and 0.25 m for D [1 mark, correct answer and unit needed]

0 2 . 1 Radio telescope site: Terrestrial and far from population centres [1 mark]. Terrestrial because large and heavy OR it needs to be far from population to avoid interference from radio waves [1 mark].

X-ray telescope site: In space [1 mark] because X-rays are absorbed by the atmosphere [1 mark].

0 2 . 2 Radio telescope detects radio waves that have longer wavelengths (~ metres) rather than X-ray wavelengths (~$10^{-9}/10^{-10}$ m) [1 mark]; collecting power proportional to diameter^2 so large for radio telescopes but very small for X-ray telescopes [1 mark]; X-rays use grazing mirrors to focus whilst radio telescopes use parabolic dish to focus [1 mark]; resolving power proportional to λ/D so small wavelength small D (X-ray) or large wavelength large D (radio) for same resolving power [1 mark].

0 3 . 1 Distance of star is proportional to $10^{\left[\frac{m-M+5}{5}\right]}$ and $(m - M + 5)$ is smaller for Procyon [1 mark] so it is closer to Earth [1 mark, second mark only awarded if first mark is correct].

0 3 . 2 Rigel: Blue star [1 mark] with helium atom and hydrogen atom absorption lines [1 mark]. Procyon: White star [1 mark] with strong absorption lines for metal ions [1 mark].

0 3 . 3 $\lambda_{max}T = 2.9 \times 10^{-3}$ m K. $T = 2.9 \times 10^{-3}/740 \times 10^{-9}$ [1 mark] $= 3900$ K (2 s.f.) [1 mark, quote your answer to a greater accuracy than the 4000 given in the question to show you have calculated it]

0 3 . 4 $I = \dfrac{P}{4\pi d^2}$ I from graph $= 4.2$ μWm^{-2} d $= 6.5 \times 9.46 \times 10^{15}$ m gives 4.2×10^{-6} $= \dfrac{P}{4\pi\left(6.5 \quad 9.46 \quad 10^{15}\right)^2}$ [1 mark]

$P = 1.996 \times 10^{29}$ W $\approx 2.0 \times 10^{29}$ W [1 mark]

$P = \sigma AT^4$ $1.9 \times 10^{29} = 5.67 \times 10^{-8}A(3900)^4$ [1 mark] $A = 1.4 \times 10^{22}$ m^2 [1 mark, allow using $T = 4000$ K (gives 1.3×10^{22} m^2), allow using $P = 2 \times 10^{29}$ Wm^{-2} for last part if P not shown (gives 1.5×10^{22} m^2 or with $T = 4000$ K gives 1.4×10^{22} m^2)]

0 4 . 1 A standard candle is an astronomical object of known intensity or known luminosity [1 mark, 'constant'/'fixed luminosity' will not be allowed], example = Type 1A supernova [1 mark, not just 'supernova', allow Cepheid variable star].

0 4 . 2 Little or no relevant information [0 marks]. One aspect partially covered [1 mark]. Two aspects partially covered [2 marks]. All three aspects partially covered, some detail missing from each OR one aspect covered and little or no information about the other two aspects [3 marks]. One aspect fully covered and two aspects partially covered OR two aspects fully covered and little or no information about the third aspect [4 marks]. Two of the three aspects fully covered with some detail missing from the third [5 marks]. All three aspects fully covered [6 marks].

In addition, for **5–6 marks** quality of communication must be good (well structured, with good spelling, punctuation and grammar). For **3–4 marks** communication must be legible and written so that the meaning can be followed. For **1–2 marks** inaccurate spelling, punctuation and grammar seriously obstructs understanding.

Aspect 1: Distance is measured by comparing the luminosity/power of a standard candle/star of known luminosity in the galaxy to the intensity received on the Earth. An inverse square law with distance relates intensity to luminosity.

Aspect 2: Doppler shift of wavelengths received from galaxy (change in wavelength/frequency of spectral lines of known wavelength) gives the velocity of the galaxy. Results showed that all the distant [must be distant] galaxies are moving away/receding.

Aspect 3: The results showed that the further away a distant galaxy was, the faster it was moving away from us. This can be explained by the fact that all distant galaxies are moving away from each other. In other words, the Universe is expanding.

Paper 3B (Medical Physics)

0 1 · 1 Diverging [1 mark]

0 1 · 2

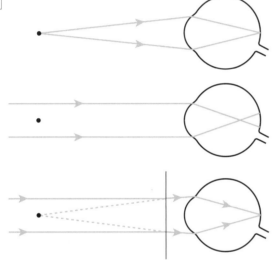

[2 marks: 1 mark for first two diagrams, 1 mark for third diagram]

0 1 · 3 $\dfrac{1}{f} = \dfrac{1}{u} + \dfrac{1}{v}$, $u = \infty$, $v = -2.5$ m

Power $= \dfrac{1}{f} = -\dfrac{1}{2.5} = -0.4$D

[1 mark for recognising that the power is negative, 1 mark for using the equation power = 1/f (allow if a wrong value for f has been calculated/written down), 1 mark for correct answer]

0 1 · 4 Cornea is not spherical [1 mark]. The image is in focus in one plane, and out of focus in the perpendicular plane [1 mark].

0 1 · 5 Cylindrical lens [1 mark]

0 2 · 1 The curve shows the intensity at each frequency that sounds equally loud [1 mark]. 0 phon = threshold of hearing [1 mark]

0 2 · 2

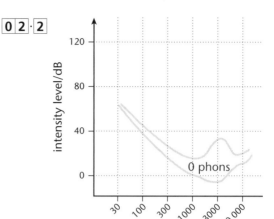

[3 marks: 1 mark for the graph above the 0 phon curve, 1 mark for a peak in the curve, after which the curve drops back close to the 0 phon curve, 1 mark for the peak at 4000 Hz, i.e. just after 3000 Hz]

0 2 · 3 In the normal aging process hearing deteriorates so you need the sound to be louder at all frequencies, but higher frequencies are affected the most [1 mark]. When hearing is damaged it usually deteriorates at all frequencies, but is usually worst at about 4000 Hz [1 mark], not at the highest frequencies [1 mark].

0 2 · 4 $I_0 = 1.0 \times 10^{-12}$ W m^{-2} [1 mark] $85 = 10 \log\left(\dfrac{I}{I_0}\right)$

so $10^{8.5} = \dfrac{I}{I_0} = \dfrac{I}{1.0 \times 10^{-12}}$ [1 mark]

$I = 3.2 \times 10^{-4}$ W m^{-2} [1 mark]

0 3 Little or no relevant information [0 marks]. One aspect partially covered [1 mark]. Two aspects partially covered [2 marks]. All three aspects partially covered, some detail missing from each OR one aspect covered and little or no information about the other two [3 marks]. One aspect fully covered and two partially covered OR two aspects fully covered and little or no information about the third [4 marks]. Two of the three aspects fully covered with some detail missing from the third [5 marks]. All three aspects fully covered [6 marks].

In addition, for 5–6 marks quality of communication must be good (well structured, with good spelling, punctuation and grammar). For 3–4 marks communication must be legible and written so that the meaning can be followed. For **1–2 marks** inaccurate spelling, punctuation and grammar seriously obstructs understanding.

Aspect 1: Patient safety: No known side effects to MR – does not use ionising radiation. But very important that there is no iron or steel or nickel in or on the patient as the magnetic fields are so strong. Can't be used for people with pacemakers and some metal implants. The X-rays used in CT scanning are ionising radiation. The dose is larger than a single X-ray. This can damage cells and there is a small risk of cancer. Unsuitable for pregnant women.

Aspect 2: Convenience: MR machines are very expensive and large. Require liquid helium for magnets, which is an extra and expensive running cost. The scans are slow to do. Machine can be claustrophobic and noisy. CT machines are also large and expensive – but cheaper than MR machines, and the scans are quicker to do. CT scans sometimes require a contrast agent such as a barium meal.

Aspect 3: Image information: MR is very good for soft tissue – especially the brain. CT scans are good for soft tissue. MR scans are poor for bones, whereas CT scans are good. MR images can give two-dimensional 'slices' at any orientation from a single scan – multiple images from a single scan. CT scan is a two-dimensional slice through the body, and requires a new scan for each image. MR has better resolution between tissue types, and gives a picture that has better resolution. MR can give real-time images. CT scan needs to rotate to produce final image.

$0\;4\cdot1$ The half life is short (six hours) so it has to be produced just before it is used **[1 mark]**.

$0\;4\cdot2$ $^{99}_{42}\mathrm{Mo} \rightarrow {}^{99}_{43}\mathrm{Tc} + {}^{0}_{-1}\mathrm{e} + \bar{v}_e$ **[2 marks: 1 mark for correct Mo, 1 mark for correct beta particle]**

$0\;4\cdot3$ Gamma radiation is emitted **[1 mark]**. A gamma camera is used to detect the radiation **[1 mark]**.

$0\;4\cdot4$ $1/T_E = 1/T_B + 1/T_p = 1/15 + 1/6 = 7/30 \; T_E$
$= 4.3$ hours (2 s.f.) **[1 mark]**

$0\;4\cdot5$ $A = A_0 e^{-\lambda t}$ $T_E = 4.3$ hours

$\lambda = \dfrac{\ln 2}{4.3 \times 3600} = 4.48 \times 10^{-5}$ **[1 mark]**

$t = 16 \times 3600$ $A = 740 \times 10^6 \times e^{-(4.48 \times 10^{-5} \times 16 \times 3600)}$ **[1 mark]**

$= 5.6 \times 10^7$ Bq $= 56$ MBq **[1 mark, ecf. value from 04.4, 2 marks for correct calculation using $T_p = 6$ hours, giving 117 MBq]**

Data and formulae booklet

DATA – FUNDAMENTAL CONSTANTS AND VALUES

Quantity	Symbol	Value	Units
speed of light in vacuo	c	3.00×10^8	m s^{-1}
permeability of free space	μ_0	$4\pi \times 10^{-7}$	H m^{-1}
permittivity of free space	ε_0	8.85×10^{-12}	F m^{-1}
magnitude of the charge of electron	e	1.60×10^{-19}	C
the Planck constant	h	6.63×10^{-34}	J s
gravitational constant	G	6.67×10^{-11}	N m^2 kg^{-2}
the Avogadro constant	N_A	6.02×10^{23}	mol^{-1}
molar gas constant	R	8.31	J K^{-1} mol^{-1}
the Boltzmann constant	k	1.38×10^{-23}	J K^{-1}
the Stefan constant	σ	5.67×10^{-8}	W m^{-2} K^{-4}
the Wien constant	α	2.90×10^{-3}	m K
electron rest mass (equivalent to 5.5×10^{-4} u)	m_e	9.11×10^{-31}	kg
electron charge/mass ratio	$\dfrac{e}{m_e}$	1.76×10^{11}	C kg^{-1}
proton rest mass (equivalent to 1.00728 u)	m_p	$1.67(3) \times 10^{-27}$	kg
proton charge/mass ratio	$\dfrac{e}{m_p}$	9.58×10^7	C kg^{-1}
neutron rest mass (equivalent to 1.00867 u)	m_n	$1.67(5) \times 10^{-27}$	kg
gravitational field strength	g	9.81	N kg^{-1}
acceleration due to gravity	g	9.81	m s^{-2}
atomic mass unit (1u is equivalent to 931.5 MeV)	u	1.661×10^{-27}	kg

ALGEBRAIC EQUATION

quadratic equation

$$x = \frac{-b \pm \sqrt{b^2 - 4ac}}{2a}$$

GEOMETRICAL EQUATIONS

arc length	$= r\theta$
circumference of circle	$= 2\pi r$
area of circle	$= \pi r^2$
curved surface area of cylinder	$= 2\pi rh$
area of sphere	$= 4\pi r^2$
volume of sphere	$= \dfrac{4}{3}\pi r^3$

ASTRONOMICAL DATA

Body	Mass/kg	Mean radius/m
Sun	1.99×10^{30}	6.96×10^8
Earth	5.98×10^{24}	6.37×10^6

Particle physics

Class	Name	Symbol	Rest energy/MeV
photon	photon	γ	0
lepton	neutrino	v_e	0
		v_μ	0
	electron	$e^\pm$	0.510999
	muon	$\mu^\pm$	105.659
mesons	π meson	$\pi^\pm$	139.576
		π^0	134.972
	K meson	$K^\pm$	493.821
		K^0	497.762
baryons	proton	p	938.257
	neutron	n	939.551

Properties of quarks

antiquarks have opposite signs

Type	Charge	Baryon number	Strangeness
u	$+\dfrac{2}{3}e$	$+\dfrac{1}{3}$	0
d	$-\dfrac{1}{3}e$	$+\dfrac{1}{3}$	0
s	$-\dfrac{1}{3}e$	$+\dfrac{1}{3}$	-1

Properties of Leptons

		Lepton number
Particles:	e^-, v_e ; μ^-, v_μ	$+1$
Antiparticles:	e^+, $\overline{v}_e$, μ^+, $\overline{v}_\mu$	-1

Photons and energy levels

photon energy	$E = hf = hc / \lambda$
photoelectricity	$hf = \phi + E_{k(max)}$
energy levels	$hf = E_1 - E_2$
de Broglie Wavelength	$\lambda = \dfrac{h}{p} = \dfrac{h}{mv}$

Waves

wave speed $\quad c = f\lambda \qquad$ period $\quad f = \dfrac{1}{T}$

first harmonic $\quad f = \dfrac{1}{2l}\sqrt{\dfrac{T}{\mu}}$

fringe spacing $\quad w = \dfrac{\lambda D}{s} \qquad$ diffraction grating $\quad d \sin \theta = n\lambda$

refractive index of a substance s, $\quad n = \dfrac{c}{c_s}$

for two different substances of refractive indices n_1 and n_2,

law of refraction $\quad n_1 \sin \theta_1 = n_2 \sin \theta_2$

critical angle $\quad \sin \theta_c = \dfrac{n_2}{n_1}$ for $n_1 > n_2$

Mechanics

moments $\qquad$ moment $= Fd$

velocity and acceleration $\qquad v = \dfrac{\Delta s}{\Delta t} \qquad a = \dfrac{\Delta v}{\Delta t}$

equations of motion $\qquad v = u + at \qquad s = \left(\dfrac{u+v}{2}\right)t$

$$v^2 = u^2 + 2as \qquad s = ut + \dfrac{at^2}{2}$$

force $\qquad F = ma$

force $\qquad F = \dfrac{\Delta(mv)}{\Delta t}$

impulse $\qquad F\,\Delta t = \Delta(mv)$

work, energy and power $\qquad W = F s \cos\theta$

$$E_k = \dfrac{1}{2}mv^2 \qquad \Delta E_p = mg\Delta h$$

$$P = \dfrac{\Delta w}{\Delta t}, \; P = Fv$$

$$\text{efficiency} = \dfrac{\text{useful output power}}{\text{input power}}$$

Materials

density $\quad \rho = \dfrac{m}{v} \qquad$ Hooke's law $\quad F = k\,\Delta L$

Young modulus $= \dfrac{\text{tensile stress}}{\text{tensile strain}}$

tensile stress $= \dfrac{F}{A}$

tensile strain $= \dfrac{\Delta L}{L}$

energy stored $\quad E = \dfrac{1}{2}F\Delta L$

Electricity

current and pd	$I = \dfrac{\Delta Q}{\Delta t}$ $V = \dfrac{W}{Q}$ $R = \dfrac{V}{I}$

resistivity

$$\rho = \frac{RA}{L}$$

resistors in series

$$R_T = R_1 + R_2 + R_3 + \dots$$

resistors in parallel

$$\frac{1}{R_T} = \frac{1}{R_1} + \frac{1}{R_2} + \frac{1}{R_3} + \dots$$

power

$$P = VI = I^2 R = \frac{V^2}{R}$$

emf

$$\varepsilon = \frac{E}{Q} \qquad \varepsilon = I(R + r)$$

Circular motion

magnitude of angular speed

$$\omega = \frac{v}{r}$$
$$\omega = 2\pi f$$

centripetal acceleration

$$a = \frac{v^2}{r} = \omega^2 r$$

centripetal force

$$F = \frac{mv^2}{r} = m\omega^2 r$$

Simple harmonic motion

acceleration

$$a = -\omega^2 x$$

displacement

$$x = A \cos(\omega t)$$

speed

$$v = \pm\omega\sqrt{(A^2 - x^2)}$$

maximum speed

$$v_{max} = \omega A$$

maximum acceleration

$$a_{max} = \omega^2 A$$

for a Mass-spring system

$$T = 2\pi\sqrt{\frac{m}{k}}$$

for a simple pendulum

$$T = 2\pi\sqrt{\frac{l}{g}}$$

Thermal physics

energy to change temperature

$$Q = mc\Delta\theta$$

energy to change state

$$Q = m\,l$$

gas law

$$pV = nRT$$
$$pV = NkT$$

kinetic theory model

$$pV = \frac{1}{3} N m (c_{rms})^2$$

kinetic energy of gas molecule

$$\frac{1}{2} m (c_{rms})^2 = \frac{3}{2} kT = \frac{3RT}{2N_A}$$

Gravitational fields

force between two masses

$$F = \frac{Gm_1 m_2}{r^2}$$

gravitational field strength

$$g = \frac{F}{m}$$

magnitude of gravitational field strength in a radial field

$$g = \frac{GM}{r^2}$$

work done

$$\Delta W = m\Delta V$$

gravitational potential

$$V = -\frac{GM}{r}$$

$$g = -\frac{\Delta V}{\Delta r}$$

Electric fields and capacitors

force between two point charges

$$F = \frac{1}{4\pi\varepsilon_0} \frac{Q_1 Q_2}{r^2}$$

force on a charge

$$F = EQ$$

field strength for a uniform field

$$F = \frac{V}{d}$$

work done

$$\Delta W = Q\Delta V$$

field strength for a radial field

$$E = \frac{1}{4\pi\varepsilon_0} \frac{Q}{r^2}$$

electric potential

$$V = \frac{1}{4\pi\varepsilon_0} \frac{Q}{r}$$

$$E = \frac{\Delta V}{\Delta r}$$

capacitance

$$C = \frac{Q}{V}$$

$$C = \frac{A\varepsilon_0\varepsilon_r}{d}$$

capacitor energy stored

$$E = \frac{1}{2}QV = \frac{1}{2}CV^2 = \frac{1}{2}\frac{Q^2}{C}$$

capacitor charging

$$Q = Q_0(1 - e^{-t/RC})$$

decay of charge

$$Q = Q_0 e^{-t/RC}$$

time constant

$$RC$$

Magnetic fields

force on a current	$F = BIl$
force on a moving charge	$F = BQv$
magnetic flux	$\Phi = BA$
magnetic flux linkage	$N\Phi = BAN \cos\theta$
magnitude of induced emf	$\varepsilon = N\dfrac{\Delta\Phi}{\Delta t}$
	$N\Phi = BAN \cos\theta$
emf induced in a rotating coil	$\varepsilon = BAN\,\omega \sin \omega t$
alternating current	$I_{rms} = \dfrac{I_0}{\sqrt{2}}$ $V_{rms} = \dfrac{V_0}{\sqrt{2}}$
transformer equations	$\dfrac{N_s}{N_p} = \dfrac{V_s}{V_p}$
	$\text{efficiency} = \dfrac{I_s V_s}{I_p V_p}$

Nuclear physics

the inverse square law for γ radiation	$I = \dfrac{k}{x^2}$
radioactive decay	$\dfrac{\Delta N}{\Delta t} = \lambda N,\ N = N_0 e^{-\lambda t}$
activity	$A = \lambda N$
half-life	$T_{1/2} = \dfrac{\ln 2}{\lambda}$
nuclear radius	$R = R_0 A^{1/3}$
energy-mass equation	$E = mc^2$

Astrophysics

1 astronomical unit = 1.50×10^{11} m

1 light year = 9.46×10^{15} m

1 parsec = 206265 AU = 3.08×10^{16} m

= 3.26 light years

Hubble constant, $H = 65$ km s^{-1} Mpc^{-1}

$$M = \frac{\text{angle subtended by image at eye}}{\text{angle subtended by object at unaided eye}}$$

in normal adjustment	$M = \dfrac{f_0}{f_e}$
Rayleigh criterion	$\theta \approx \dfrac{\lambda}{D}$
magnitude equation	$m - M = 5 \log\dfrac{d}{10}$
Wien's law	$\lambda_{max} T = 2.9 \times 10^{-3}$ m K
Stefan's law	$P = \sigma A T^4$
Schwarzschild radius	$R_s \approx \dfrac{2GM}{c^2}$
Doppler shift for $v \ll c$	$\dfrac{\Delta f}{f} = -\dfrac{\Delta\lambda}{\lambda} = \dfrac{v}{c}$
red shift	$z = -\dfrac{v}{c}$
Hubble's law	$v = Hd$

Medical physics

lens equations	$P = \dfrac{1}{f}$
	$m = \dfrac{v}{u}$
	$\dfrac{1}{f} = \dfrac{1}{u} + \dfrac{1}{v}$
threshold of hearing	$I_0 = 1.0 \times 10^{-12}$ W m^{-2}
intensity level	$\text{intensity level} = 10 \log\dfrac{I}{I_0}$
absorption	$I = I_0 e^{-\mu x}$
	$\mu_m = \dfrac{\mu}{\rho}$
ultrasound imaging	$Z = pc$
	$\dfrac{I_r}{I_i} = \left(\dfrac{Z_2 - Z_1}{Z_2 + Z_1}\right)^2$
half-lives	$\dfrac{1}{T_E} = \dfrac{1}{T_B} + \dfrac{1}{T_P}$